Art Projects Made Easy

D1715829

Art Projects Made Easy
Recipes for Fun

LINDA J. ARONS
Oakland Unified School District
Oakland, California

Illustrated by
LINDA J. ARONS

Graphic Design by
CATHY MEDEIROS
"Words To Go, Etc."

1995
TEACHER IDEAS PRESS
A Division of
Libraries Unlimited, Inc.
Englewood, Colorado

AFX0046

Copyright © 1995 Linda J. Arons
All Rights Reserved
Printed in the United States of America

No part of this publication may be reproduced, stored in a retrieval system, or transmitted, in any form or by any means, electronic, mechanical, photocopying, recording, or otherwise, without the prior written permission of the publisher. An exception is made for individual library media specialists and teachers, who may make copies of activity sheets for classroom use in a single school. Other portions of the book (up to 15 pages) may be copied for in-service programs or other educational programs in a single school.

Curric
372.5
A825

TEACHER IDEAS PRESS
A Division of Libraries Unlimited, Inc.
P.O. Box 6633
Englewood, CO 80155-6633
1-800-237-6124

Library of Congress Cataloging-in-Publication Data

Arons, Linda J.
  Art projects made easy : recipes for fun / Linda J. Arons ; illustrated by
  Linda J. Arons ; graphic design by Cathy Medeiros.
    xv, 165 p. 17x25 cm.
    Includes bibliographical references and index.
    ISBN 1-56308-342-6
    1. Art--Study and teaching (Elementary) I. Title.
  N350.A825 1995
  372.5'044--dc20   95-35158
                                                        CIP
                                                        Rev.

OLSON LIBRARY
NORTHERN MICHIGAN UNIVERSITY
MARQUETTE, MICHIGAN 49855

CONTENTS

INTRODUCTION

RECIPES

APPETIZERS (Art Principles)

SALADS AND VEGETABLES (Collage)

BREAD MAKING (Crafts)

MAIN DISHES (Drawing)

CAKES AND DECORATING (Painting)

with thanks to

Adam Arons
Micah Arons
Gloria Durflinger
Amy Edgerley
Ginger Hom
Elaine Kohn
Andrea Mitchell
Edie Wilson
Marian Wilson
Marlene Wilson
Ann Yamoto

and special thanks to

Michael Hopkins
for inspiring me to write this cookbook

Cathy Medeiros
for her professional assistance

Jason Cook
for his patience and guidance

Dear Teachers,

This art cookbook has been designed for the teacher who desires a fun and effective art lesson. Most of the art recipes in this book are simple and easy to follow. In addition, many of them require ingredients and utensils that most schools have in stock. If you're thinking that you never seem to have the time to organize and complete an effective art lesson, this cookbook is for you. Most of the recipes are easy to set up, with many designed to be completed in one fifty-minute period.

A good art lesson should not only provide fun for your students but should also include a simple goal—that each student will complete the project following the outlined instructions. If this is accomplished, the art lesson will have been a success.

Have your students strive for creativity in each lesson. I tell my students that they should, if possible, try to create art that stems from their *own* ideas, not from the ideas of their classmates, nor from the "example" art that I show them.

Be objective when evaluating a student's work. In grading, I use the following four criteria:

1. How well did the student follow the outlined instructions?
2. Technically, how well was the project executed?
3. Were the student's ideas original and creative?
4. Did the student make good use of time and complete the project?

Classroom "critiques" can be very helpful in evaluating students' work. After completing a project, display their work so that it is visible to everyone. Then discuss each student's project (include principles of art, originality, technical merit, etc.). Students will gain a great deal of insight into their art from this technique.

It is my hope that these recipes will not only be helpful but will also spark additional ideas for enhancing your classroom curriculum and art program. Please be sure to modify any or all of the recipes to fit the needs of your students.

Have fun and enjoy!

Linda

Introduction

Recipe Format

This art cookbook consists of sixty-seven recipes within eight chapters. Each recipe includes the following sections:

Cooking Terms

These are the vocabulary words associated with each lesson.

Ingredients/Utensils

These are the materials required for each lesson. In most cases, the type of paper (if paper is required) is listed first, followed by the remaining materials.

Directions

These are the procedures that you and your students should follow.

Tasting Critique

These are suggested questions to ask yourself when evaluating a student's work.

Stirring In the Curriculum

These are methods of integrating the lesson with other areas of your curriculum. References to children's picture books (in terms of the illustrator's style) are often listed here.

What Shall We Cook Up Tomorrow?

These are additional art activities that are extensions of the original lesson.

The illustrations in each recipe have been designed to give you a clearer understanding of the lesson. However, they should be used mainly as catalysts for creating art that is original.

Use of Ingredients/Utensils

Colored Chalk

Using chalk or charcoal is a lot of fun, but it can be messy. Applying a spray fixative on the finished product helps to prevent smearing.

Colored Pencils

These are great for creating detailed drawings. Older students often prefer these to crayons.

Crayons

Have your students try to blend the various colors. Also, have them try to use more than one value (shade) by varying the pressure of the crayon on the paper.

Glue

I prefer Elmer's® white glue to paste. If containers or lids are not available, pass out small pieces of paper and have each student make a "gluebox," which will keep the glue from running onto their desks or tables. Then pour a little glue into each box. I tell my students to use only one finger for applying the glue.

Marking Pens

Students love using them (older students prefer fine-tipped pens, but these wear out quickly if used to fill large areas). Certain brands last longer than others—Mr. Sketch® is one of these. A nice effect is to outline with pens and fill in with crayons, which conserves the life of the marking pens.

Oil Pastels

These are similar to crayons but different in that they are brighter. They show up very well on colored paper. However, oil pastels wear down more quickly than crayons.

Scissors

Some students tend to cut using the tip of the scissors rather than the inside edges of the blades. I tell my students that the "crocodile" should never close its mouth completely. This prevents "trapping" the paper and also allows for better cutting control.

Tempera Paints

These are great for teaching students about mixing colors. Providing the colors red, yellow, blue, black, and white will allow students to create many "new" colors. You do, however, need lots of containers.

Watercolor Paints

These are practical because they don't require additional containers, nor as much cleanup time, as tempera paints; just the paints, newspaper, "mixing paper" (used in place of a palette), water containers, and brushes. Watercolor paints can be applied lightly (with more water) to create a "wash" effect, or heavily (with less water) to create a darker effect.

Cooking Suggestions

Creativity lovers might think of a photocopier as a no-no. However, I have found it to be very helpful when used to provide "structure" for a lesson. Using a photocopy as a *guide* to accompany a lesson (where students draw their own interpretations of the photocopied image) can be very helpful for the "I can't draw" student. Another good catalyst is the use of a photocopied image that shows only half of a picture, which students are asked to complete.

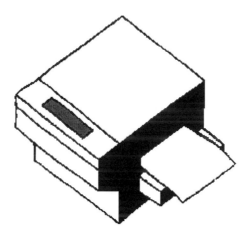

Presentation of Recipes

Paper Framing (Matting)

Framing a picture does wonders! Even the most ordinary-looking artwork can appear very attractive once it has been framed. Choosing the right colors can make a big difference in the work's final appearance. Often, a thin (1/4"–1/2") border surrounded by a wider border (2"–3") can make the picture stand out. A three-dimensional effect can be created by placing the artwork on paper that is about 1" larger on all sides, folding the sides inward, and pinching together the corners of the border paper.

Bulletin Boards

As with framing, an attractive bulletin board can make the most ordinary-looking artwork appear outstanding. Every bulletin board should have a title, and it is important to choose a background color that will enhance the appearance of the frames and the artwork. Attractive positioning of the artwork is also important.

Cooking Principles

The following are a few basic principles that are simple to follow and, if applied, will enhance the results of your students' work:

Color   Use of tints, tones, and shades can add richness to a picture. Students tend to restrict themselves to using only pure hues.

Composition Use of the entire page can create an aesthetically pleasing picture. Have students try to avoid drawing all their objects at the bottom of their picture.

Contrast Use of shading can be extremely effective in most pictures. Students often tend to restrict themselves to the use of one value (shade) of each color.

Depth   Use of the illusion of depth in a picture (created by including a "front," "middle," and "back") can add realism. Have students try to avoid drawing all their objects "in a row."

Dominance Use of main shapes and colors can play an important role in good design.

Land   *Water*

Horizon Line Use of a horizon line can add realism.

Perspective Use of depth can enhance a picture. Two-dimensional objects can be easily converted to three-dimensional objects.

Size Variation Use of different sizes for shapes and objects can add interest to a picture.

Texture Use of lines to create a visual and tactile surface appearance can enhance a picture.

APPETIZERS
(Art Principles)

APPETIZERS
(Art Principles)

Line Design

Cooking Terms

curve	intersect	overlap	thin	wiggly
diagonal	line	straight	vertical	zigzag
horizontal	narrow	thick	wide	

Ingredients/Utensils

- 12"-x-18" sheets of black and white construction paper
- 1/2"–1" strips of black and white construction paper
- Glue
- Scissors

Directions

Teacher:

- Discuss the definition of *line* (a collection of points having a beginning and an end).
- Discuss types of lines (thick, thin, straight, curved, wiggly, zigzagged, long, short, etc.).

Student:

- Cut black or white strips to form various types of lines.
- Glue black lines on white paper or white lines on black paper to form a picture or design.

Line Design
cont.

Tasting Critique
- Did the student experiment with different types of lines?
- Does the finished project show good design?
- Was it done neatly?

Stirring In the Curriculum
- Brainstorm on lines in the real world (tree branches, telephone wires, television antennae, leaf veins, etc.).
- Do a creative writing lesson entitled "If I Were a Line . . ."
- Refer to *Harold and the Purple Crayon* by Crockett Johnson, in which the illustrations are done using a continuous line.

What Shall We Cook Up Tomorrow?
- Add the element of color by using strips of colored paper.

APPETIZERS
(Art Principles)

Circle Art

Cooking Terms

arc   intersect
circle   overlap
concentric   shape
dominant

Ingredients/Utensils
- Construction paper (size and color can vary)
- Pencils
- Scissors
- Glue
- Various sizes of circles for tracing (lids, heavy paper, tagboard, etc.

Directions

Teacher:
- Discuss the definition of *circle* (a closed curve, every point of which is of equal distance from a fixed point inside the curve).
- Discuss the following circle placements:
    1. not touching
    2. touching
    3. overlapping
    4. concentric

- Discuss the use of *dominance* (using several circles of a specific size).

4

Circle Art
cont.

Directions (*cont.*)

Student:

- Trace circles onto construction paper (having only one color of paper available will allow students to focus on the element of shape).
- Cut out circles.
- Glue circles onto a different color of construction paper using various circle placements.

Tasting Critique

- Is there variation in size of circles?
- Was a dominant size chosen?
- Does the finished project show good design?
- Was it done neatly?

Stirring In the Curriculum

- Brainstorm on circles in the real world (tires, doughnuts, buttons, the moon, the sun, etc.).
- Do a creative writing lesson entitled "If I Were a Circle . . . "
- Refer to *Round & Round & Round* by Tana Hoban, which depicts everyday objects that are in circular form.

What Shall We Cook Up Tomorrow?

- "Circle Art" can be done by drawing or drawing and coloring circles. Designs can also be added to the circles.
- This process may be done using other shapes (squares, rectangles, triangles, etc.) or a combination of shapes.
- Holiday shapes such as hearts, shamrocks, and pumpkins make nice designs.

1	2	3	4	5	6	7	8	9

Value Scale

Value Painting

Cooking Terms

black	gray	value
contrast	middle gray	value scale
dominant	neutrals	white

Ingredients/Utensils

- 12"-x-18" sheets of white paper
- Black and white tempera paints
- Paintbrushes
- Water containers
- Mixing paper (used in place of a palette)

Directions

Teacher:

- Discuss the definition of *value* (degree of lightness or darkness in a color), and the use of value scales (1–9; 5 is middle gray), contrast, neutrals, and dominant value.
- Show samples of value scales, if possible.
- Demonstrate how to mix paint. Always begin with white and add black unless mixing a very dark gray (this saves paint).
- Demonstrate how to achieve the proper consistency of paint. It should not be too thick nor too thin.

Value Painting
cont.

Directions (*cont.*)

Student:

- Draw a picture or design of what will be painted.
- Paint the entire paper. Remember to use mixing paper to mix the various values and to rinse paintbrush well when changing values.

Tasting Critique

- Does the paint show good consistency?
- Does the painting show good composition?
- Was the student able to mix various values?
- Was a dominant value chosen?

Stirring In the Curriculum

- Compare a value scale to a musical scale.
- Refer to *The Garden of Abdul Gasazi* by Chris Van Allsburg, in which the illustrations depict excellent use of value.

What Shall We Cook Up Tomorrow?

- Try doing value painting using one hue (monochromatic) and neutrals (black, white, and grays).

APPETIZERS
(Art Principles)

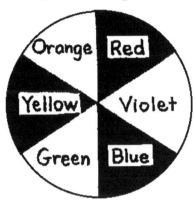

▲ = *Primary Colors*
△ = *Secondary Colors*

Color

Cooking Terms

color wheel   primary
hue   secondary

Ingredients/Utensils
- 9"-x-12" sheets of white construction paper
- 12"-x-18" sheets of white construction paper
- Paintbrushes
- Red, yellow, and blue tempera paints
- Paint containers
- Water containers
- Mixing paper (used in place of a palette)

Directions
Teacher:
- Discuss color wheels and the three primary colors (red, yellow, and blue), from which the secondary colors (green, orange, and violet) and other colors are made.

8

Color

cont.

Directions (*cont.*)

Student:

- On a practice sheet of 9"-x-12" white paper, mix two primary colors at a time to discover the secondary colors.
- Using a sheet of 12"-x-18" white paper, paint a picture using the primary colors. Mixing paper can be used in place of a palette.

Tasting Critique

- Can the student name the primary colors and know which primary colors create each secondary color?
- Did the student mix the secondary colors?

Stirring In the Curriculum

- Use in conjunction with a science unit on light to show that sunlight passing through a prism produces a spectrum or rainbow of colors.
- Do a creative writing lesson entitled "My Favorite Color."
- Refer to *Color Dance* by Ann Jonas or to *Mouse Paint* by Ellen Walsh, in which both the stories and illustrations depict color mixing.

What Shall We Cook Up Tomorrow?

- Discover the tertiary colors by mixing each primary color with an adjacent secondary color on the color wheel (e.g., red-violet, blue-green, yellow-orange, etc.).
- Create tints by adding white to each color.
- Create shades by adding black to each color.
- Create tones by adding the complement (opposite color on the color wheel) to each color.

APPETIZERS
(Art Principles)

Cool border (blue, green, violet, etc.) →

← *Warm center (red, yellow, orange, etc.)*

Cool-Warm Painting

Cooking Terms

border	neutral	pattern
cool	opposite	warm

Ingredients/Utensils

- 9"-x-12" sheets of white paper
- Crayons
- Paintbrushes
- Pencils
- Rulers
- Watercolor paints
- Water containers

Directions

Teacher:

- Discuss warm colors (yellows, oranges, reds, pinks, browns, etc.) and cool colors (blues, greens, violets, etc.).
- Discuss the use of *repeat patterns*.
- Using a ruler, draw a 1" border around each sheet of paper (older students can do this themselves).

Cool-Warm Painting
cont.

Directions (*cont.*)
Student:
- Design a border. Create a repeat pattern using pencil and crayons. Use either cool or warm colors.
- Create a picture that is centered inside the border using pencil and watercolor paints or crayons. Use warm colors (and neutrals, if desired) if the crayon border is composed of cool colors, and cool colors if the crayon border is composed of warm colors.

Tasting Critique
- Does the border pattern repeat?
- Were accurate colors used in the border?
- Were accurate colors used in the center?
- Was the picture well drawn and painted/colored?

Stirring In the Curriculum
- Brainstorm on objects in the real world that are cool or warm (the ocean, the sun, ice cubes, fire, etc.).
- Refer to *Land of the Long White Cloud: Maori Myths, Tales and Legends* by Kiri Te Kanawa, in which the illustrations are done using cool and warm colors.

What Shall We Cook Up Tomorrow?
- Try doing other pictures or greeting cards with different borders.

APPETIZERS
(Art Principles)

Texture Plates

Cooking Terms

plate   repeat   texture

Ingredients/Utensils
- 12"-x-18" sheets of white construction paper
- 12"-x-18" sheets of construction paper or board (color can vary)
- Pencils
- Rulers
- Crayons or marking pens
- Scissors
- Glue

Directions
Teacher:
- Discuss the definition of *texture* (the visual or tactile surface appearance of something) and show examples (rug samples, toothbrush, sandpaper, glass, sponge, etc.).
- Use the chalkboard to show how different lines create different textures.

Student:
- On a sheet of 12"-x-18" white paper, rule out six or eight 4"-x-4" or 5"-x-5" squares (for younger students, teachers may either do this themselves or else provide a template).
- Draw a repetition of dots and lines inside each square to create texture plates.
- Trace the dots and lines with crayons or marking pens.

Texture Plates
cont.

Directions (*cont.*)
- Cut out the texture plates.
- Glue an attractive arrangement onto a sheet of 12"-x-18" construction paper.

Tasting Critique
- Did the student create a variety of textures?
- Was the work done neatly?

Stirring In the Curriculum
- Use in conjunction with a science unit on the five senses.
- Classify objects as rough or smooth.
- Refer to *Is It Rough? Is It Smooth? Is It Shiny?* by Tana Hoban, which depicts everyday objects that are textured.
- Refer to books by Keizaburo Tejima (*The Bear's Autumn*, *Fox's Dream*, *Owl Lake*, *Woodpecker Forest*, etc.), in which the illustrations are done with lines that create different textures.

What Shall We Cook Up Tomorrow?
- Have student select one texture plate and do an enlargement on a sheet of 9"-x-12" white paper.

APPETIZERS
(Art Principles)

Symmetry Name Design

Cooking Terms
balance   reverse   symmetry

Ingredients/Utensils
- 9"-x-12" sheets of white construction paper
- Pencils
- Crayons or marking pens
- Black marking pens

Directions
Teacher:
- Discuss the definition of *symmetry* (the correspondence in size, form, and arrangement of parts on opposite sides of a plane, line, or point) in nature, shapes, and objects.
- On the chalkboard, demonstrate what happens when letters are "flipped" (reversed). Some letters do not change (such as I/i, O/o, T/t, and X/x); others do (such as B/b, E/e, K/k, N/n, and S/s).

Student:
- Fold a sheet of 9"-x-12" white construction paper in half lengthwise.
- With a pencil, write your name in large letters that "rest" on the fold. Press hard enough to make an impression on the back side of the bottom half (*Fig. A*).
- Unfold the paper and rotate it to a vertical position.
- With a pencil, trace each letter on the left and the right side of the fold (*Fig. B*).

fold → Fig. A

Fig. B *fold ↓*

14

Symmetry Name Design
cont.

Directions (*cont.*)
- Trace the pencil lines with a black marking pen.
- Add lines to connect the letters (*Fig. C*). Remember, whatever is drawn on one side must be drawn on the other.

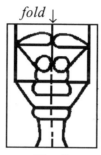

fold ↓

Fig. C

- Color the design with crayons or marking pens, using the same colors on both sides of the fold. Add designs inside some or all of the shapes. When complete, your name does not have to be recognizable.

Tasting Critique
- Is the design symmetrical?
- Is there detail in the design?
- Was the work done neatly?

Stirring In the Curriculum
- Brainstorm on objects in the real world that are symmetrical (leaves, flowers, masks, furniture, butterflies, etc.).
- Refer to *Upside-Downers* by Mitsumasa Anno (pp. 24–25), in which the illustration depicts symmetry.

What Shall We Cook Up Tomorrow?
- Upper-grade students can use cursive for their names.
- Try writing name on edge of folded black paper. Cut out name (keeping paper folded), unfold name, and glue it on white paper; then color.

APPETIZERS
(Art Principles)

One-Point Perspective Drawing

Note: This recipe is really not that difficult. Give it a try!

Cooking Terms

background	foreground	radiate
distance	perspective	vanishing point

Ingredients/Utensils
- Drawing paper (size can vary)
- Pencils
- Rulers

Directions

Teacher:
- Discuss the definition of *perspective* (the technique representing natural objects on a flat surface as they appear to the eye).
- Show sample pictures or photographs, if possible.
- On the chalkboard, demonstrate how to draw a one-point perspective picture.

Student:
- Mark one point (the "vanishing point") on a sheet of paper.
- Draw lines that radiate out from the point (*Fig. A*).

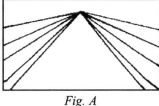 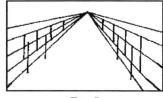

Fig. A	*Fig. B*

- Add vertical lines (*Fig. B*), where appropriate, to create sides of buildings, fence posts, telephone poles, tree trunks, and so on.

16

One-Point Perspective Drawing
cont.

Directions (*cont.*)
- Add horizontal lines (*Fig. C*) to form the fronts and tops of buildings.

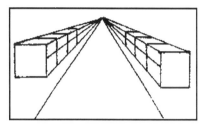

Fig. C

- Add detail such as trees, plants, doors, windows, and sidewalks (*Fig. D*).

Fig. D

Tasting Critique
- Does the picture seem to recede into the distance?
- Was the picture drawn well?

Stirring In the Curriculum
- Use in conjunction with a social science unit on Ancient Egypt by comparing the two-dimensional drawing technique used in Egyptian art to three-dimensional perspective drawings.
- Study famous artists who use or have used perspective in their work (Canaletto, Raphael, M. C. Escher, etc.).

What Shall We Cook Up Tomorrow?
- Take students outside to draw buildings in perspective.

SALADS AND VEGETABLES
(Collage)

SALADS AND VEGETABLES
(Collage)

Texture Collage (Paper Only)

Note: An excellent recipe for all ages!

Cooking Terms

collage   dominance   overlap   texture

Ingredients/Utensils
- 9"-x-12" or 12"-x-18" sheets of heavy paper
- Various types of paper, with both visual and tactile textures (magazine, newspaper, tissue paper, wallpaper, wrapping paper, corrugated paper, aluminum foil, etc.)
- Scissors
- Glue

Directions

Teacher:
- Discuss the definition of *collage* (assorted materials glued or pasted to a surface to make a picture or design).
- Discuss the definition of *texture* (see teacher directions, page 12), and show examples of various types of textured paper.
- Discuss the dominance, placement, and overlapping of paper pieces.

Texture Collage (Paper Only)
cont.

Directions (*cont.*)

Student:

- Tear or cut paper into pieces. Vary the size, shape, and color, keeping dominance in mind.
- Glue the paper pieces onto background paper to make a design. Pieces may overlap one another.

Tasting Critique

- Was the work done neatly?
- Was dominance of size, shape, and/or color used?

Stirring In the Curriculum

- Refer to *Anno's Italy* by Misumasa Anno, *The Carolers* by Georgia Guback, or *Sundiata: Lion King of Mali* by David Wisniewski, in which the illustrations are done as cut-paper collages.

What Shall We Cook Up Tomorrow?

- Use paper pieces to make collage pictures (objects, scenes, etc.).

SALADS AND VEGETABLES
(Collage)

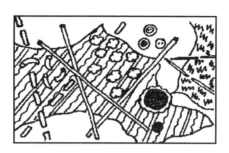

Mixed-Media Collage

Cooking Terms

collage   recycle   scrap   texture

Ingredients/Utensils
- Scissors
- Glue
- Assorted collage materials (toothpicks, soda straws, macaroni, bottle caps, buttons, pebbles, scraps of fabric, textured paper, etc.)
- Cardboard (size should depend on amount of items collected)
- Crayons or paints (optional)

Directions

Teacher:
- Discuss the definitions of *texture* and *collage* (see teacher directions, pages 12 and 20, respectively).
- Brainstorm ideas for how each collage material might be used.

Mixed-Media Collage
cont.

Directions (*cont.*)

Student:

- Arrange some or all of the collage materials into a design or picture.
- When you are satisfied with the design, glue the items onto cardboard.
- If desired, use crayons or paint to add any necessary detail.

Tasting Critique

- Does the finished product show good design?
- Was it done neatly?
- If representational, can the objects be recognized?

Stirring In the Curriculum

- Use in conjunction with a science unit on conservation by identifying recyclable objects.

What Shall We Cook Up Tomorrow?

- Try doing single-material collages such as all fabric, all toothpicks, etc.

SALADS AND VEGETABLES
(Collage)

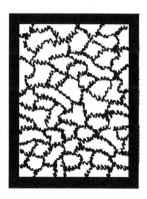

Torn Tissue Paper Collage

Cooking Terms

    collage   overlap   transparent

Ingredients/Utensils
- Sheets of white construction paper (size can vary)
- Sheets of black construction paper
- Colored tissue paper
- White glue
- Paintbrushes
- Water containers
- Shellac

Directions

Teacher:
- Discuss the possible results that can be achieved by overlapping colors of tissue paper.

Student:
- Tear tissue paper into various shapes.
- With a paintbrush, stroke a mixture of glue and water over each sheet of tissue paper onto a sheet of white construction paper.

Torn Tissue Paper Collage
cont.

Directions (*cont.*)
- Continue applying tissue until either the entire paper is covered with tissue or until a desired picture or design is completed.
- Let the collage dry for at least one hour.
- Apply shellac.
- Frame the collage with black construction paper.

Tasting Critique
- Is the picture or design pleasing?
- Was the overlapping technique used?

Stirring In the Curriculum
- Incorporate into any language arts, science, or social science unit by using themes or subjects related to your unit of study (plants, farm scenes, storybook scenes, etc.).
- Refer to *Six Crows* by Leo Lionni, in which some of the illustrations are done with torn paper.

What Shall We Cook Up Tomorrow?
- Shapes may be cut instead of torn.
- Shapes may be outlined with a black marking pen.

25

OLSON LIBRARY
NORTHERN MICHIGAN UNIVERSITY
MARQUETTE, MICHIGAN 49855

SALADS AND VEGETABLES
(Collage)

Paper Mosaics

Cooking Terms

chip	narrow	square	uniform
mosaic	space	tile	

Ingredients/Utensils

- 9"-x-12" sheets of construction paper (color can vary)
- 3" squares of construction paper (colors can vary)
- Pencils
- Scissors
- Glue
- Empty egg cartons for separating and storing pieces of colored paper

Directions

Teacher:

- Discuss the definition of *mosaics* (fitting pieces of material together to fill a flat surface).
- Discuss the origin or history of mosaics.
- Discuss the use of mosaics.
- Display samples, if possible.

Student:

- On a sheet of 9"-x-12" construction paper, draw a large and simple picture or design (flowers, a fish, a head, etc.).

Paper Mosaics
cont.

Directions (*cont.*)
- Using precut 3" squares of construction paper, cut mosaic pieces into mosaic "chips" (approximately 1/2" x 1/2"), sort them by color, and place them into an egg carton for storage.
- Glue the mosaic chips onto a sheet of construction paper, leaving a narrow space of background color between each piece.
- Continue gluing until the entire paper is covered with chips.

Tasting Critique
- Does the picture have a mosaic appearance?
- Is the subject recognizable?
- Are the pieces fairly evenly separated?

Stirring In the Curriculum
- Study countries or cultures that are known for their work in mosaics (Aztecs, Byzantine Empire, Greeks, Romans, Mayans, modern Mexico, etc.).

What Shall We Cook Up Tomorrow?
- Try creating dot mosaic art using a hole puncher for making circles in place of squares.
- Use other forms of paper for mosaic pieces (magazines, newspaper, wrapping paper, etc.).

SALADS AND VEGETABLES
(Collage)

Rectangle Reversals

Cooking Terms

positive/negative space   reverse   shape

Ingredients/Utensils

- 9"-x-12" sheets of black construction paper
- 5"-x-7" sheets of construction paper (assorted colors)
- Pencils
- Scissors
- Glue

Directions

Teacher:

- Discuss positive/negative space.
- Demonstrate how to cut out and "flip" or "split" shapes (see *Fig. B*).

Student:

- Draw various shapes (two per side) along four sides of 5"-x-7" white or colored paper so that the edge of the paper forms one side of each shape (*Fig. A*).

Fig. A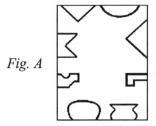

- Cut out shapes carefully and save each piece.
- Glue the remains of the rectangle onto black paper. (Be sure to center it.)

Rectangle Reversals
cont.

Directions (*cont.*)
- Return each shape to its original position (like doing a puzzle) and either "flip" or "split" it. Older students may enjoy doing double and triple flips, double and triple splits, or a combination of both (*Fig. B*).

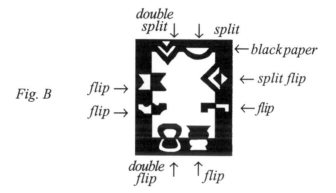

Fig. B

- Glue each shape onto the black paper to form a design that uses positive/negative space (*Fig. B*).

Tasting Critique
- Was the work done neatly?
- Were the shapes flipped and split correctly?

Stirring In the Curriculum
- Use in conjunction with a geometry lesson on congruency.
- Refer to *Round Trip* by Ann Jonas, in which the illustrations depict positive/negative space.

What Shall We Cook Up Tomorrow?
- Give a theme to each design (cut out trees for Christmas, hearts for Valentine's Day, flowers, letter shapes, etc.).

SALADS AND VEGETABLES
(Collage)

Positive/Negative-Space Repeat Patterns

Cooking Terms

alternate	negative space	shape
motif	positive space	

Ingredients/Utensils
- 9"-x-12" sheets of construction paper (color can vary)
- 3" squares of construction paper (24 per student—12 of one color and 12 of another color)
- Pencils
- Scissors
- Glue

Directions
Teacher:
- Discuss positive/negative space.
- Show examples so students will understand the difficulty in distinguishing positive space from negative space and vice versa.

Student:
- On a sheet of 9"-x-12" construction paper, glue twelve 3" squares, alternating two colors to create a checkerboard effect.
- On another 3" square, draw an interesting shape or motif that incorporates positive/negative space. Be sure the shape or motif touches at least two sides of the 3" squares.

Positive/Negative-Space Repeat Patterns
cont.

Directions (*cont.*)
- Trace the shape or motif onto the remaining eleven squares.
- Cut out the eleven shapes or motifs.
- Glue each shape onto a 3" square, alternating colors (see the illustration at the beginning of this recipe). Shapes may be flipped, if desired.

Tasting Critique
- Is the design attractive?
- Did the student correctly incorporate positive/negative space?

Stirring In the Curriculum
- Use in conjunction with a mathematics unit on measurement by having students divide their paper into squares.
- Refer to *Ida's Idea* by Wendy Kindred, and to *Modern Geometric Design* by Adolf Lorch, both of which contain illustrations depicting positive/negative space and repeat patterns.

What Shall We Cook Up Tomorrow?
- Use holiday or seasonal motifs (pumpkins, hearts, snowmen, etc.).
- Try drawing and coloring the shapes in place of cutting and gluing.
- For the very advanced, try cutting out both the positive and negative shapes and piecing them together like a puzzle.

SALADS AND VEGETABLES
(Collage)

Yarn Pictures

Cooking Terms
collage   texture

Ingredients/Utensils
- 10"–20" lengths of yarn
- Cardboard or tagboard (stiff paper can be substituted)
- Scissors
- Glue
- Pencils

Directions
Teacher:
- Discuss the definition of *collage* (see teacher directions, page 20).
- Decide on a plan or design for the project, such as holiday motifs (hearts or pumpkins), circles (see the recipes "Circle Art," page 4, and "African Circle Art," page 114), spring flowers, and so on.

Student:
- Using pencil on cardboard or tagboard, draw a design or picture that includes such things as holiday motifs, circles, and spring flowers.
- Apply glue along 3"– 4" of pencil line at a time, placing the yarn on top of the glue line. Cut the yarn where necessary.

Yarn Pictures
cont.

Directions (*cont.*)
- Continue this process until the entire picture is outlined.
- Fill in the centers with yarn pieces, going in different directions to create varying textures. Cut the yarn to fit where necessary. Remember to apply glue a little at a time to prevent it from drying too soon.

Tasting Critique
- Does the finished project show good design and composition?
- If representational, can the objects be recognized?
- Was it done neatly?

Stirring In the Curriculum
- Incorporate into any language arts, science, or social science unit by using themes or subjects related to your unit of study (maps, portraits of famous people, storybook pictures, etc.).

What Shall We Cook Up Tomorrow?
- Yarn gluing can be used to make greeting cards or as a craft to cover bottles, jars, cans, and boxes.

SALADS AND VEGETABLES
(Collage)

Stained Glass

Note: Great for window display!

Cooking Terms

    border   stained-glass windows

Ingredients/Utensils
- 9"-x-12" sheets of black construction paper
- 1"-wide strips of black construction paper
- Tissue paper or cellophane (assorted colors)
- Scissors
- Glue
- Pencils

Directions

Teacher:
- Discuss the definition of *stained-glass windows* (windows made up of separate pieces of colored glass that form a picture or design).
- Discuss the origin or history of stained-glass windows.
- Discuss the use of stained-glass windows.
- Display samples or pictures of stained glass or samples of paper-collage stained glass.

Stained Glass
cont.

Directions (*cont.*)

Student :
- On a sheet of 9"-x-12" black construction paper, make a large and simple line drawing of an object (a face, an animal, a building, etc.) that touches all four sides of the paper.
- Widen all lines by drawing a second line 3/8"–1/2" away from and parallel to each original line (thereby "doubling" the width of all lines).
- Cut out the picture, cutting between the parallel lines.
- Place pieces of colored tissue paper or cellophane over all cutout areas and trace each shape a little larger than the actual shape.
- Cut out the shapes.
- Glue the shapes onto the backside of black paper until all cutout areas are covered.

Frame:
- Cut out four strips of 1"-wide black construction paper to form a frame around the picture. The frame must overlap the picture slightly.
- Glue frame sides together.
- Place the frame over the picture and glue it down at points where it overlaps the picture.

Tasting Critique
- Is the overall effect pleasing?
- Was the chosen subject conducive to stained glass?
- Were the black border lines well drawn and cut out?

Stirring In the Curriculum
- Incorporate into any language arts, science, or social science unit by using themes or subjects related to your unit of study (landmarks, mammals, tropical rain forests, etc.).
- Study famous artists who are known for their work in stained glass (Marc Chagall, Georges Rouault, Louis C. Tiffany, etc.).

What Shall We Cook Up Tomorrow?
- Create stained-glass Christmas pictures.

BREAD MAKING
(Crafts)

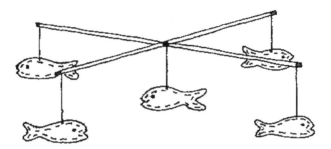

Paper Mobiles

Cooking Terms

color	mobile	shape	three-dimensional
dowel	pattern	theme	

Ingredients/Utensils

- Newsprint
- Newspaper
- Marking pens
- Scissors
- Crayons
- Pencils
- Staplers
- String
- Wooden dowels

Directions

Teacher:

- Display a sample mobile and discuss its characteristics (shape, color, pattern, movement, three-dimensional aspect, etc.).
- Discuss various theme possibilities (shapes, animals, fish, babies, people, etc.).

Student:

- Fold a sheet of newsprint in half.
- Draw or trace a figure on the newsprint.

38

Paper Mobiles
cont.

Directions (*cont.*)
- Color both sides of the figure with crayons or marking pens.
- Cut out the figure.
- Stuff the figure with newspaper and staple closed along its edges.
- Repeat the above steps, making four more figures.
- Tie two dowels together with string to form a cross.
- Fasten string at the top of the figures and attach them to dowels (one at each end of each dowel and one at the center of the cross).

Tasting Critique
- Was an original theme chosen?
- Were figures well drawn and colored?

Stirring In the Curriculum
- Incorporate into any language arts, science, or social science unit by using themes or subjects related to your unit of study (healthy foods, the solar system, storybook characters, etc.).

What Shall We Cook Up Tomorrow?
- Make mobiles using other materials (paint, wire, foil, construction paper).
- Try making miniature mobiles using Popsicle^{TM} sticks in place of doweling and suspending miniature figures.

BREAD MAKING
(Crafts)

Foil Pictures

Note: These make a gorgeous display—very impressive!

Cooking Terms

aluminum foil   permanent   relief

Ingredients/Utensils

- 9"-x-12" pieces of cardboard
- Aluminum foil
- String
- Glue
- Masking tape
- Permanent marking pens

Directions

Teacher:
- Cut pieces of aluminum foil.
- Demonstrate the technique for using permanent marking pens on aluminum foil, stressing not to recolor any areas.

Student:
- Make a simple drawing on cardboard with pencil, or glue a picture of a simple subject onto cardboard.
- Glue string onto the cardboard, following the main lines of the drawing or picture.

Foil Pictures
cont.

Directions (*cont.*)
- Let the glue dry.
- Lay a piece of aluminum foil over the cardboard (the foil must extend beyond the cardboard by at least 1" on all sides).
- Holding the aluminum foil in place, turn over the cardboard.
- Gently pull the aluminum foil until it is tight and smooth across the front.
- Fold the foil edges down and tape them to the back of the cardboard.
- Turn the cardboard face-up again and press down on the foil over the entire picture so the string "ridges" stand out, giving a relief effect.
- Color all sections and the background with permanent marking pens, being careful not to recolor any areas. When finished, there should be no bare foil showing.

Tasting Critique
- Is the overall effect pleasing?
- Was the picture drawn well?
- Was the string and foil placed neatly?
- Was the picture colored accurately?

Stirring In the Curriculum
- Incorporate into any language arts, science, or social science unit by using themes or subjects related to your unit of study (African jungle life, Mexico, mythological figures, etc.).

What Shall We Cook Up Tomorrow?
- A stained-glass window effect looks great using this technique.

BREAD MAKING
(Crafts)

Paper Bag Puppets

Note: Puppet "themes" can be holiday-oriented, integrated with a unit of study, "free choice," and so on.   Ideas are endless!

Cooking Terms
> features   flap   puppet

Ingredients/Utensils
- Paper bags
- Pencils
- Crayons
- Construction paper (varied sizes and colors)
- Glue
- Face patterns (optional)
- Fabric, yarn, buttons, foil, glitter, and other decorative materials

Directions
Teacher:
- Display a sample paper bag puppet and demonstrate how it "talks" (use a hand inside the bag to open and close the flap).

Student:
- Place a paper bag in front of you so the flap side is toward the front and at the top (*Fig. A*).

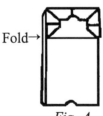
Fig. A

Fig. B

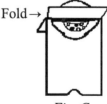
Fig. C

- On construction paper, draw a face (do not include a mouth or a chin), or use a face pattern as a guide.
- Color, cut out, and glue the face onto the flap of the paper bag (*Fig. B*).

42

Paper Bag Puppets
cont.

Directions (*cont.*)

- On construction paper, draw a mouth and a chin, or use a face pattern as a guide.
- Color, cut out, and glue the mouth and the chin under the flap (*Fig. C*). When the flap is down, the mouth should be hidden, but the chin should show.

Fig. D   *Fig. E*   *Fig. F*

- Add hair by gluing yarn to the face (*Fig. D*).
- Add additional features (hat, jewelry, glasses, eye patch, mustache, freckles, etc.) appropriate to the puppet's character and personality (*Fig. E*).
- Draw a body on the paper bag below the face (*Fig. F*).
- Color or add various types of paper or fabric. Be creative!

Tasting Critique

- Was the puppet assembled neatly?
- Were the student's ideas original?

Stirring In the Curriculum

- Incorporate a puppet show into any language arts, science, or social science unit by using themes or subjects related to your unit of study (conservation, proper safety practices, storybook characters, etc.).

What Shall We Cook Up Tomorrow?

- Try making other types of puppets (stick, sock, finger, etc.). Refer to *Puppets* by Lyndie Wright.

BREAD MAKING
(Crafts)

Toothpick Sculptures

Cooking Terms
    balance   sculpture   square   triangle

Ingredients/Utensils
- 6" squares of waxed paper
- Glue
- Flat toothpicks
- Paint, tissue paper, glitter, and other decorative materials (optional)

Directions
Teacher:
- Discuss sculpture in terms of balance and dimension.

Student:
- Form a shape (triangle, square, etc.) with toothpicks and glue it to waxed paper. (The more sides the shape has, the more toothpicks will be needed to create the finished sculpture.)
- Dip the ends of the toothpicks into glue (using very little) and begin building up a shape (continue with the original shape or change it as desired).
- When the sculpture is complete, pull it from the waxed paper and complete the bottom side.
- Let the sculpture dry.
- (Optional) Decorate with paint, tissue paper, glitter, and so on.

Toothpick Sculptures
cont.

Tasting Critique
- Is the sculpture well balanced?
- Does the sculpture look good from all sides?
- Was the work done neatly?

Stirring In the Curriculum
- Use in conjunction with mathematics lessons on shapes, counting, parallel lines, etc.
- Study famous artists who are known for their work in sculpture (Brancusi, Michelangelo, Auguste Rodin, etc.).

What Shall We Cook Up Tomorrow?
- Combine toothpicks and marshmallows to make sculptures. Put glue on end of toothpick and push into marshmallow.

BREAD MAKING
(Crafts)

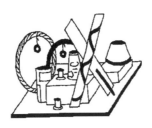

Junk Sculptures

Note: Provide the materials and just let your students go!

Cooking Terms

| balance | build | rotate | sculpture |
| base | junk | scraps | three-dimensional |

Ingredients/Utensils
- Pieces of cardboard large enough to form bases for the sculptures
- Glue
- Assorted "junk" objects (spools, lids, bottle caps, egg cartons, cans, pieces of wood, toilet paper rolls, styrofoam cups, etc.)
- Paint (optional)

Directions
Teacher:
- Discuss sculpture in terms of its three-dimensional aspect, its balance, and its aesthetics.
- Place junk objects on a table at the front or center of the classroom.

Student:
- Begin gluing junk objects onto a piece of cardboard.
- Continue adding objects, building the sculpture as high and as wide as desired. Remember to rotate the sculpture every so often to check for balance from all angles.
- (Optional) Paint the sculpture.

Junk Sculptures
cont.

Tasting Critique
- Does the sculpture appear to be well thought out?
- Does the sculpture show good balance and design?

Stirring In the Curriculum
- Use in conjunction with a science unit on conservation by identifying recyclable objects.
- Study famous artists who are known for their work in sculpture (Alexander Calder, Michelangelo, Henry Moore, etc.).

What Shall We Cook Up Tomorrow?
- Try creating sculptures using just one medium, such as toothpicks, straws, Popsicle™ sticks, little boxes, and so on.

BREAD MAKING
(Crafts)

Ceramic Leaf Prints

Cooking Terms

ceramic	kiln	print	texture
clay	nature	properties	vein
fire	pattern	repeat	

Ingredients/Utensils

- 12"-x-18" or 18"-x-24" sheets of manila paper to protect surfaces
- Ceramic clay
- Water containers
- Variety of fresh leaves with stems
- Scissors (optional)
- Glaze (optional)
- Paintbrushes (optional)

Directions

Teacher:

- Discuss the origin and history of clay.
- Discuss the properties of clay (distinguishing clay from sand and other soils).
- Discuss texture and pattern.
- Use string to divide clay into chunks for students.
- Place manila paper on working surfaces.

Student:

- Roll and knead clay.
- Flatten clay until it is approximately 1/4" thick.

Ceramic Leaf Prints
cont.

Directions (*cont.*)
- Form clay into a nice shape (if not cutting out leaf shape), adding water when necessary.
- Press a leaf (vein side down) and its stem into the clay.
- (Optional) Cut out the leaf print, cutting around the edge of the leaf and stem (make the clay stem large to avoid breakage). Lift the leaf from the clay.
- Allow clay to dry for a week or two before firing.
- Glaze, if desired, and fire.

Tasting Critique
- Is the leaf's texture easy to see?
- Are the edges smooth?
- Were the shaping and cutting done well?

Stirring In the Curriculum
- Use in conjunction with a science unit on plants.
- Compare to plant fossils.
- Refer to *Fossil*, a volume in the Eye Witness Series, by Paul D. Taylor, which depicts several illustrations of plant fossils.

What Shall We Cook Up Tomorrow?
- Design a bowl or dish using leaf prints.

BREAD MAKING
(Crafts)

Ceramic Bowls (Coiled)

Note: Most students really enjoy working with clay. Before beginning this recipe, have them explore this artistic medium.

Cooking Terms

ceramic	fire	knead
clay	glaze	pottery
coil	kiln	

Ingredients/Utensils

- 12"-x-18" or 18"-x-24" sheets of manila paper to protect surfaces
- Ceramic clay
- Water containers
- Toothpicks or other carving tools
- Glaze (optional)
- Paintbrushes (optional)

Directions

Teacher:

- Discuss the origin and history of clay.
- Discuss the properties of clay (distinguishing clay from sand and other soils).
- Use string to cut the clay into chunks for students.
- Place manila paper on working surfaces.

Student:

- Roll and knead the clay.
- Roll a fairly large piece of clay between the palms of your hands until a long rope (about 1/4" thick) is formed.

Ceramic Bowls (Coiled)
cont.

Directions (*cont.*)
- Coil the rope to form the base of a bowl (*Fig. A*).

Fig. A   *Fig. B*   *Fig. C*   *Fig. D*

- Build the wall of the bowl to a desired height and width (*Fig. B*).
- Smooth clay so coils are no longer visible (*Fig. C*).
- Carve designs or figures into the sides of the bowl (*Fig. D*) using toothpicks or other carving tools.
- Allow clay to dry for a week or two before firing.
- Glaze, if desired, and fire.

Tasting Critique
- Is bowl fairly level and smooth?
- Are the carvings attractive?
- Did student roll out rope evenly?

Stirring In the Curriculum
- Use in conjunction with a social science unit on Native Americans.
- Refer to *Ceramics* by Elizabeth Constantine and Lewis Krevolin, which depicts photographs of coiled pots and vases.

What Shall We Cook Up Tomorrow?
- Explore other methods for making bowls.

BREAD MAKING
(Crafts)

Stitchery

Cooking Terms
back stitch	running stitch	stretch
needle	sew	

Ingredients/Utensils
- 12"-x-12" pieces of burlap (size can vary)
- Pencils
- Drawing paper
- Marking pens
- Masking tape
- Sewing needles
- Yarn
- Scissors

Directions
Teacher:
- On a piece of burlap, demonstrate the "running stitch" and/or the "back stitch" (depending on the grade level of students).

Student:
- Practice stitching on scrap pieces of burlap.
- Draw a picture on drawing paper of the picture to be stitched.
- Copy the picture onto a piece of burlap (a marking pen works best).

Stitchery
cont.

Directions (*cont.*)
- Use the following guidelines when sewing:
    1. Cut a piece of yarn about 18" in length.
    2. Tie a knot at one end and thread a needle at the other end.
    3. Insert the needle into the burlap from the backside.
    4. Keep stitches small (1/2" maximum length).
    5. Always end on the backside so knots won't show.
    6. When tying a knot, use the needle to push the knot down until it touches the burlap.
    7. Stitch the border first (this prevents the burlap edges from fraying). Then stitch the picture outline (older students can fill in the picture outline using the backstitch).

Tasting Critique
- Are all the stitches approximately the same size?
- Was the student able to work independently?
- Was it done neatly?

Stirring In the Curriculum
- Incorporate into any language arts, science, or social science unit by using themes or subjects related to your unit of study (flags, storybook scenes, U.S. states, etc.).
- Combine pieces together to make wall hangings.

What Shall We Cook Up Tomorrow?
- Try using holidays such as Christmas or Mother's Day as stitchery themes.

MAIN DISHES
(Drawing)

MAIN DISHES
(Drawing)

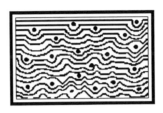

Dot-Line Drawing

Note: For a little discipline, don't miss this one!

Cooking Terms

arc	dot	line
control	horizontal	parallel

Ingredients/Utensils
- 5"-x-8" or 6"-x-9" sheets of white paper (no lines)
- Colored marking pens (preferably fine-tipped) or colored pencils

Directions

Teacher:
- Tell students they will be practicing control in the making of lines.
- On the chalkboard, demonstrate how to do dot-line drawing.

Student:
- Mark many dots (twenty to thirty) at random on a sheet of paper.
- Using a pencil or marking pen, and starting at the top of the paper, draw a horizontal line across the paper from edge to edge. When reaching a dot, go around it (above or below).

Dot-Line Drawing
cont.

Directions (*cont.*)
- Draw each line as close and as parallel as possible to the one above or below it, without touching or crossing the lines.
- Continue making lines, varying colors as desired, until the paper is filled.

Tasting Critique
- Are all the lines parallel?
- Are the lines horizontal?
- Are the colors pleasing?
- Was the student able to control the lines so they did not touch?

Stirring In the Curriculum
- Use in conjunction with a mathematics lesson on parallel lines.

What Shall We Cook Up Tomorrow?
- Try other forms of dot-line drawing using curved, zigzag, and scalloped lines.

MAIN DISHES
(Drawing)

Contour Drawing

Note: A great opportunity to practice hand-eye control.

Cooking Terms

contour   line   outline   silhouette

Ingredients/Utensils
- Drawing paper (size can vary)
- Pencils, crayons, or charcoal
- Drawing boards (optional)

Directions

Teacher:
- Discuss the definition of *silhouette* (the outline of a figure filled in with black).
- Discuss the definition of *contour* (the outline of a figure or object). Compare to *silhouette*.
- Display sample contour drawings.
- Discuss and display various subject possibilities.
- On the chalkboard, demonstrate how to draw contours.

Student:
- Select a subject.
- Draw an outline of the subject, keeping your eyes on the subject and trying not to go off the paper with your drawing utensil.

Contour Drawing
cont.

Directions (*cont.*)
- Move to another subject and repeat the previous step, using either another sheet of paper or another area of the original paper.
- Continue drawing as desired. Do not be concerned with the final composition of the picture.

Tasting Critique
- How well do the drawings resemble the original subjects?
- Was the student able to stay on the paper?
- Were the lines connected at appropriate places?

Stirring In the Curriculum
- Incorporate into any language arts, science, or social science unit by using objects or subjects related to your unit of study (butterflies, leaves, map work, etc.).

What Shall We Cook Up Tomorrow?
- Try going outside in search of subjects.

MAIN DISHES
(Drawing)

sitting   *stretching*   *marching*

Stick Figure Drawing

Cooking Terms

action   figure   movement
charcoal   motion

Ingredients/Utensils
- Charcoal paper or drawing paper
- Pencils, crayons, or charcoal

Directions

Teacher:
- On the chalkboard, demonstrate how to draw stick figures by using an oval for the head and lines for the body, arms, and legs.
- Select a student model to hold an action pose (throwing a ball, marching, kicking, stretching, etc.).
- Select additional student models as desired.

Student:
- Using charcoal paper or drawing paper, draw a stick figure in the same pose as the model, using an oval for the head and lines for the body, arms, and legs.
- Continue practicing drawing stick figures using other student models posing in different positions.
- Practice drawing stick figures *without* using a model.

Stick Figure Drawing
cont.

Tasting Critique
- Did the student correctly capture the actions displayed by the models?
- Did the student create his or her own actions?

Stirring In the Curriculum
- Use in conjunction with a language arts lesson by writing dialogue or captions to comic strips done using stick figures.
- Study cave drawings done by early humans.

What Shall We Cook Up Tomorrow?
- Add simple articles of clothing to the stick figures.
- Draw cartoons or comic strips using stick figures.

MAIN DISHES
(Drawing)

Partner Portraits

Cooking Terms

likeness   portrait   proportion

Ingredients/Utensils
- 9"-x-12" sheets of white paper
- Pencils
- Crayons, colored chalk, colored pencils, charcoal, oil pastels, or other drawing materials

Directions

Teacher:
- Discuss the definition of *portrait* (a likeness of a person, especially of the face).
- Display examples, such as school photos, that show the face and shoulder area only.
- Have students choose partners and face each other.

Student:
- Draw what you see, beginning with your partner's eyes, and then draw the nose, mouth, hair, face, and shoulders.
- Color the drawing, using accurate colors, if possible.

Partner Portraits
cont.

Tasting Critique
- Is there a likeness to the partner?
- Was good proportion used?

Stirring In the Curriculum
- Study famous artists who are known for their portrait art (Frans Hals, Rembrandt, van Gogh, etc.).
- Refer to the Art for Children Series by Ernest Raboff, and to the Getting to Know the World's Greatest Artists Series by Mike Venezia, both of which discuss and illustrate the works of famous artists.

What Shall We Cook Up Tomorrow?
- Using mirrors, do self-portraits.

MAIN DISHES
(Drawing)

Still-Life Drawings

Cooking Terms

background   elliptical   inanimate
composition   foreground   overlap

Ingredients/Utensils

- Still-life objects (vases, flowers, fruit, bowls, teapots, salt and pepper shakers, etc.)
- 9"-x-12" sheets of white paper
- Pencils
- Crayons, chalk, or oil pastels

Directions ·

Teacher:

- Place a table(s) in the room easily visible to all students.
- Arrange objects on table(s), either in a row so that students can create their own composition or in a pleasing arrangement.
- Using art prints of still lifes, discuss the definition of a *still life* (a picture of inanimate objects).
- Discuss the definition of *composition* (see "Cooking Principles," page xv).

Still-Life Drawings
cont.

Directions (*cont.*)
Student:
- Draw a still life, making sure to use good composition (draw objects large enough to fill the entire paper), overlap objects, use elliptical shapes where necessary, and show a table or some type of resting place for the objects (see the illustration at the beginning of this recipe).
- Color with crayon, chalk, or oil pastels.

Tasting Critique
- Did the student use good composition?
- Were the objects drawn accurately?

Stirring In the Curriculum
- Study famous artists who are known for their still lifes (Braque, Cézanne, Matisse, etc.).
- Refer to the Art for Children Series by Ernest Raboff, and to the Getting to Know the World's Greatest Artists Series by Mike Venezia, both of which discuss and illustrate the works of famous artists.

What Shall We Cook Up Tomorrow?
- Try doing still lifes using other media (watercolor paints, tempera paints, yarn, cut paper, etc.).

MAIN DISHES
(Drawing)

Magazine Art

Note: Students love this recipe. Be sure to try it!

Cooking Terms

asymmetric	horizontal	symmetric
diagonal	reproduce	vertical

Ingredients/Utensils
- Construction paper
- Glue
- Magazine pictures
- Mixing paper (used in place of a palette)
- Oil pastels
- Pencils
- Scissors

Directions
Teacher:
- Explain the objective of this lesson: to draw and color the "missing" half of a magazine picture so that the magazine art resembles the complete magazine picture as closely as possible.

Student:
- Select a magazine picture that you would like to draw.
- Cut the picture into the shape of a rectangle, square, or circle.
- Fold the picture in half (horizontally, vertically, or diagonally).

Magazine Art
cont.

Directions (*cont.*)
- Cut the picture in half along the fold.
- Glue one half of the picture onto a sheet of white paper.
- Place the other half back in its original position next to the half that is glued and trace its sides with a pencil.
- Remove the traced half and try to reproduce it using pencil.
- Color the pencil picture with oil pastels. (Use a separate sheet of white paper to mix and test colors so that they match those in the magazine picture. Make sure the colors are dark enough.)

Tasting Critique
- Does the student's half look like the original?
- Do the colors match?

Stirring In the Curriculum
- Incorporate into any language arts, science, or social science unit by using themes or subjects related to your unit of study (city and country life, Egypt, insects, etc.).

What Shall We Cook Up Tomorrow?
- Using a photocopy of half of a figure or picture, have students reproduce the other half. Cartoon characters work well using this technique.
- Using an entire magazine picture, have students reproduce it so that it resembles the picture as closely as possible.

MAIN DISHES
(Drawing)

Product Design

Cooking Terms

advertise	logo	slogan
company	product	

Ingredients/Utensils

- 9"-x-12" sheets of white paper
- Pencils
- Crayons or colored pencils

Directions

Teacher:

- Discuss advertising art using sample products (cereals, cosmetics, cleaning products, snack items, etc.) that show good visual designs, and display logos and slogans.

Student:

- Using an entire sheet of paper as the front of a box, jar, or container, create a design that includes the following:
    1. A picture of the product or something related to the product
    2. An *original* name for the product, with original lettering
    3. A company logo or symbol
    4. An original slogan (not "the more you eat, the more you want," etc.)
- Color the design.

Product Design
cont.

Tasting Critique
- Were all four requirements included in the project?
- Were the ideas original?
- Was good layout and design used?

Stirring In the Curriculum
- Use in conjunction with various mathematics, language arts, or social science units by visiting a local supermarket to learn more about advertising, budgeting, price comparisons, and so on.

What Shall We Cook Up Tomorrow?
- Try doing this project in three dimensions. Draw a box layout (*Fig. A*) using a lightweight board such as tagboard. Be sure to include "tabs" to connect the sides. Draw and color design. Cut and fold to form a box.

Fig. A

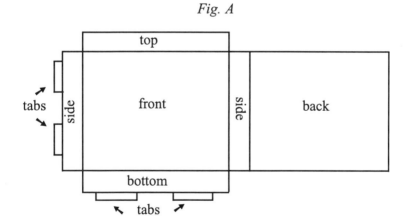

MAIN DISHES
(Drawing)

Framed Pictures

Cooking Terms
    border   frame   repeat

Ingredients/Utensils
- 9"-x-12" sheets of white paper
- 11"-x-14" sheets of white paper
- Pencils
- Crayons or marking pens
- Rulers
- Scissors
- Masking tape

Directions

Teacher:
- Display a sample or use the chalkboard to illustrate framed pictures (pictures with a repeat-pattern border).

Student:
- Draw any picture on a sheet of 9"-x-12" white paper.
- Color the picture with crayons or marking pens.
- Make a frame as follows:
    1. On a sheet of 11"-x-14" paper, use a ruler to draw a rectangle (8-3/4" x 11-3/4").
    2. Cut out the rectangle.
    3. Place the remaining frame (2-1/4" wide) over the picture and center it.
    4. Lightly tape the inside corners of the frame to the picture.

Framed Pictures
cont.

Directions (*cont.*)

5. Flip the picture over and securely tape the frame to the picture. Turn the picture back over and remove the tape from the inside corners.
6. Decorate the frame with repeating pictures or designs that connect, in some way, with picture theme (e.g., a "flowered" frame for a spring picture, a "cactus" frame for a desert picture, a "pumpkin" frame for a Halloween picture, etc.).
7. Color the frame. (A marking-pen frame contrasts nicely with a crayon-colored picture.)
8. (Optional) Fold the frame sides forward and pinch the corners to create a three-dimensional effect.

Tasting Critique
- Do the designs or pictures on the frame repeat?
- How well does the frame theme match the picture?
- Was the picture drawn well?

Stirring In the Curriculum
- Incorporate into any language arts, science, or social science unit by using themes or subjects related to your unit of study (Japan, outer space, reptiles, etc.).
- Refer to *Wolf's Favor* by Fulvio Testa, in which the illustrations are outlined with repeat-pattern borders.

What Shall We Cook Up Tomorrow?
- Make framed pictures for special occasions (birthdays, holidays, thank-yous, etc.).

CAKES AND DECORATING
(Painting)

CAKES AND DECORATING
(Painting)

Scribble Art

Cooking Terms

abstract	design	realism	scribble
closed figure	intersect	texture	

Ingredients/Utensils

- 9"-x-12" to 12"-x-18" sheets of white paper
- Pencils
- Black crayons
- Watercolor paints
- Paintbrushes
- Water containers
- Mixing paper (used in place of a palette)

Directions

Teacher:

- Discuss how different designs seem to create different textures.
- Discuss abstract art, comparing it to realism.

Student:

- Draw a scribble design with pencil on a sheet of white paper, making sure the design has no loose ends.
- Trace over the pencil with a black crayon.
- Using watercolor paints, paint each section of the drawing with different designs. Paint some sections with solid colors, if desired.

Scribble Art

cont.

Tasting Critique
- Is the overall appearance pleasing?
- Was the painting done neatly?
- Were different designs and textures used?

Stirring In the Curriculum
- Use in conjunction with a geometry lesson on closed figures or line intersection.
- Study famous artists who are known for their work in abstract art (Juan Gris, Paul Klee, Picasso, etc.).
- Refer to the Art for Children Series by Ernest Raboff, and to the Getting to Know the World's Greatest Artists Series by Mike Venezia, both of which discuss the works of famous artists.

What Shall We Cook Up Tomorrow?
- Do a scribble art painting using a stick and rubber cement. Let rubber cement dry, paint over it, and pull off the rubber cement after paint has dried. (See the recipe "Rubber Cement Painting," page 88.)

CAKES AND DECORATING
(Painting)

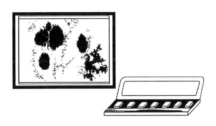

Wet Watercolor Designs

Cooking Terms

blend   blob   tilt

Ingredients/Utensils
- Watercolor paper
- Newspaper
- Watercolor paints
- Paintbrushes
- Water containers

Directions

Teacher:
- Discuss and demonstrate what happens when watercolor paints are used on a wet surface, tilting a sheet of paper in different directions to create various designs.

Student:
- Use a paintbrush to cover an entire sheet of paper with clear water. Paper should be quite wet.
- Dip the paintbrush into paint and put blobs on the wet paper. Use several colors.
- Tilt the paper in different directions to form different designs. Experiment with different papers and colors.

76

Wet Watercolor Designs
cont.

Tasting Critique
- Were interesting designs created?
- Which colors blended well? Which did not?

Stirring In the Curriculum
- Refer to *Crow Chief* by Paul Goble and *Follow Me!* by Nancy Tafuri, in which some of the illustrations are done with a wet watercolor technique.

What Shall We Cook Up Tomorrow?
- Outline designs with marking pens.
- Mount or frame designs for display.
- Make designs on paper large enough to use as book covers.
- Assemble a class mural using each student's work.

CAKES AND DECORATING
(Painting)

Painting to Music

Cooking Terms

broken	image	pitch	tempo
curve	line	rhythm	wavy
direction	movement	stroke	

Ingredients/Utensils

- Watercolor paper
- Newspaper to protect working surfaces
- Watercolor paints
- Paintbrushes
- Water containers
- Mixing paper (used in place of a palette)
- Records, tapes, or CDs with various rhythms

Directions

Teacher:
- Discuss music in terms of variations in sound, pitch, rhythm, and tempo.
- Discuss the relationship of music to lines (i.e., music can make us imagine lines that are long, short, thin, thick, wavy, straight, broken, etc.).
- Discuss the relationship of music to image and color.
- Play sample records or tapes.
- Play the first record or tape.

Painting to Music
cont.

Directions (*cont.*)
Student:
- Use your imagination and paint to the music. Try to correlate brush strokes and line movements with the music. Do not overpaint.
- Try creating another painting.

Tasting Critique
- Does the picture correlate with the music?
- Did the student use variations of lines and strokes?

Stirring In the Curriculum
- Use in conjunction with a music lesson or songs that students know.
- Study the musician who wrote the music that is used for this recipe.

What Shall We Cook Up Tomorrow?
- Try *drawing* to music using crayons.

CAKES AND DECORATING
(Painting)

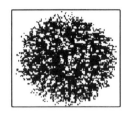

Sponge Painting

Cooking Terms

dab	print	texture
pattern	shape	

Ingredients/Utensils
- Paper (type, size, and color can vary)
- Tempera paints
- Paint containers (lids work well)
- Sponge pieces (shape can vary)
- Extra paper for testing

Directions

Teacher:
- Demonstrate the technique for creating a sponge painting by gently dipping a sponge piece into paint and dabbing paint onto testing paper. Make sure students see that using too much paint doesn't work.

Student:
- Dip a sponge piece into paint and make a test print on testing paper.
- Gently dab the sponge piece onto the paper to make a print.
- Continue in this manner, overlapping prints and using various colors and sponge shapes to produce a complete picture or design.

Sponge Painting
cont.

Tasting Critique
- Is the overall effect pleasing?
- Was the right amount of paint used to make each print?

Stirring In the Curriculum
- Refer to *Whistle for Willie* by Ezra Jack Keats, in which some of the illustrations are done using a sponge painting technique.

What Shall We Cook Up Tomorrow?
- Now that your students have had a chance to dabble in dabbing, assign a more specific recipe—that of making greeting cards by using heart shapes for Valentine's Day or Mother's Day, shamrock shapes for St. Patrick's Day, tree shapes for Christmas, etc.
- Combine sponge painting with crayon or cut paper to create a picture or design.

CAKES AND DECORATING
(Painting)

Straw Painting

Cooking Terms

branch	spread	wander
random	straw	

Ingredients/Utensils

- White or light-colored construction paper
- Soda straws
- Tempera paints
- Paintbrushes

Directions

Teacher:

- Discuss painting techniques that do not require a paintbrush (finger, stick, sponge, string, etc.). Warn students that blowing hard over an extended period of time may cause headaches.

Student:

- Using a paintbrush, drop paint onto white or light-colored construction paper.
- Place one end of a straw directly above the paint and blow gently. The paint should spread out into thin lines.
- Continue dropping paint and blowing through the straw until the picture is complete.

Straw Painting
cont.

Tasting Critique
- Does the picture resemble something in particular?
- Can the lines be controlled somewhat by the blowing?

Stirring In the Curriculum
- Do a creative writing lesson entitled "My Straw Painting Reminds Me of . . ."

What Shall We Cook Up Tomorrow?
- Make straw paintings on other types of paper (wallpaper, wrapping paper, colored tissue paper, etc.).
- Make cherry blossom trees using the straw painting technique for the branches and pink tissue paper for the blossoms.

CAKES AND DECORATING
(Painting)

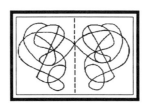

String Painting

Cooking Terms

press   print   symmetry

Ingredients/Utensils

- Heavy paper (size can vary)
- String or yarn (lengths can vary)
- Tempera paints
- Paint containers

Directions

Teacher:

- Discuss the definition of *symmetry* (see teacher directions, page 14).

Student:

- Fold a sheet of heavy paper in half.
- Dip a piece of string into paint.
- Run your fingers along the string, without squeezing, to remove excess paint. (Too much paint will create a smeared effect.)
- Open the paper and arrange the string on one half.
- Fold the other half of the paper over the string and press firmly with your hand.

String Painting
cont.

Directions (*cont.*)
- Open the paper and carefully remove the string.
- Repeat this process, if desired, using the same piece of string dipped into the same color or another piece of string dipped into another color.

Tasting Critique
- Was the proper amount of paint used?
- Were interesting designs and shapes formed?

Stirring In the Curriculum
- Brainstorm on objects in the real world that are symmetrical (butterflies, flowers, leaves, masks, etc.).
- Use in conjunction with a geometry lesson on congruency.

What Shall We Cook Up Tomorrow?
- Do string painting over geometric forms that have been glued to paper.

CAKES AND DECORATING
(Painting)

Paint-Yarn Pictures

Cooking Terms

object	relief	yarn
outline	shellac	

Ingredients/Utensils
- White construction paper or any heavy paper (size can vary)
- Pencils
- Watercolor paints
- Paintbrushes
- Water containers
- Black yarn (color can vary)
- Scissors
- Shellac (optional)

Directions
Teacher:
- Demonstrate the "paint-yarn" technique.

Student:
- On a sheet of white construction paper, draw with pencil a large and simple picture of an object, scene, or design (vase with flowers, butterfly, clown's head, etc.).
- Paint the picture with watercolor paints.

Paint-Yarn Pictures
cont.

Directions (*cont.*)
- (Optional) On the back of the picture, paint a 1"-wide strip at each end of the paper with shellac. (This will keep the paper from warping.)
- Let the picture dry.
- Outline the main areas of the picture with glue and yarn, creating a relief effect.

Tasting Critique
- Is the overall effect pleasing?
- Was the picture kept simple?
- Was the picture drawn well?
- Was the painting done neatly?

Stirring In the Curriculum
- Incorporate into any language arts, science, or social science unit by using themes or subjects related to your unit of study (map work, noun pictures, storybook pictures, etc.).

What Shall We Cook Up Tomorrow?
- Use this "paint-yarn" technique on greeting cards or holiday art.

CAKES AND DECORATING
(Painting)

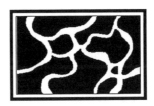

Rubber Cement Painting

Cooking Terms

accidental	resist	rubber cement
controlled	rub	

Ingredients/Utensils
- 12"-x-18" sheets of white construction paper
- Newspaper
- Small sticks
- Rubber cement
- Small containers
- Tempera paints (thinly mixed)
- Paintbrushes

Directions

Teacher:
- Demonstrate the "rubber-cement painting" technique.

Student:
- Using a stick dipped into rubber cement, draw a picture or design on a sheet of 12"-x-18" white paper. Make thick and thin lines as you go.
- Let the picture dry for ten minutes.
- Paint over the dried rubber cement with a large paintbrush.

Rubber Cement Painting
cont.

Directions (*cont.*)
- Let the paint dry.
- Pull off the rubber cement by rubbing with your fingers, leaving a design of white lines.

Tasting Critique
- Does the picture or design exhibit good composition?
- If a design was drawn, does it appear to have been planned and controlled or merely accidental?
- Was the painting done neatly?

Stirring In the Curriculum
- Incorporate into any language arts, science, or social science unit by using themes or subjects related to your unit of study (ocean life, plants, storybook pictures, etc.).

What Shall We Cook Up Tomorrow?
- Try this technique using spray bottles filled with food coloring and water in place of paint.

COOKIES
AND CANDIES
(Holidays and
Seasonal Art)

COOKIES AND CANDIES
(Holidays and Seasonal Art)

Autumn Trees

Cooking Terms
autumn   print   tone
dab   texture

Ingredients/Utensils
- 9"-x-12" sheets of construction paper (color can vary)
- Pencils
- Crayons
- Tempera paints
- Paint containers (lids work well)
- Sponge pieces
- Extra paper for testing prints

Directions
Teacher:
- Prepare paint for leaves using autumn colors and tones (yellow, orange, red, violet, brown, etc.).
- Demonstrate the technique for creating a sponge painting by gently dipping a sponge piece into paint and dabbing paint onto testing paper. (Make sure students see that using too much paint doesn't work.)

Student:
- On a sheet of construction paper, draw tree trunk(s) with branches.
- Color the trunk(s) and branches with crayons.

Autumn Trees
cont.

Directions (*cont.*)
- Dip a sponge piece into paint and make a test print on testing paper.
- Gently dab the sponge onto the paper to form leaves.
- Continue in this manner, changing colors as desired.

Tasting Critique
- Is the overall effect pleasing?
- Were the tree trunks and branches drawn well?
- Was each leaf print made with the right amount of paint?

Stirring In the Curriculum
- Use in conjunction with a social science unit on autumn.
- Use in conjunction with a science unit on trees.
- Refer to *Fall* by Ann Blades, in which the illustrations depict autumn trees.

What Shall We Cook Up Tomorrow?
- Use this "sponge-leaf" technique to illustrate spring flowers and leaves.

COOKIES AND CANDIES
(Holidays and Seasonal Art)

Pumpkin-Head Characters

Cooking Terms

accent	facial	imagination
character	fringe	trace

Ingredients/Utensils
- 6"-x-9" sheets of orange construction paper
- 6"-x-9" sheets of black construction paper
- Photocopies depicting a pumpkin (pumpkin should be about 6" x 5")
- Scissors
- Crayons
- Glue
- Additional paper to make bodies (optional)

Directions
Teacher:
- Discuss ideas for pumpkin-head characters (cat, clown, spider, witch, vampire, baseball player, cartoon character, etc.).

Student:
- Cut out a photocopy of a pumpkin (older students may draw their own).
- Trace the pumpkin onto a sheet of orange construction paper.
- Add lines to the pumpkin, if desired.

94

Pumpkin-Head Characters
cont.

Directions (*cont.*)
- Draw face parts and accessories (eyes, nose, whiskers, hat, jewelry, bow, etc.) on a sheet of black construction paper.
- Cut out the face parts (paper can be curled, fringed, and folded to create hair, eyelashes, a hat, etc.).
- Glue the face parts onto the pumpkin.
- Add crayon marks for accent.
- (Optional) Create a body for the pumpkin.

Tasting Critique
- Is the character recognizable?
- Was the work done neatly?
- Were the student's ideas original?

Stirring In the Curriculum
- Have students do a creative writing lesson about their pumpkin-head character.
- Incorporate into any language arts, science, or social science unit by using themes or subjects related to your unit of study (famous people, mammals, storybook characters, etc.).

What Shall We Cook Up Tomorrow?
- Design witch heads using a squash shape in place of a pumpkin shape.

COOKIES AND CANDIES
(Holidays and Seasonal Art)

Tissue Paper Turkeys

Cooking Terms

collage	rough	texture
relief	smooth	

Ingredients/Utensils
- 9"-x-12" sheets of paper
- 1" squares of colored tissue paper
- Crayons
- Glue
- Pencils
- Photocopies depicting a turkey (optional)

Directions

Teacher:
- Demonstrate the "tissue paper" techniques.

Student:
- Draw a turkey with pencil on a sheet of paper (if desired, use a photocopy as a guide).
- Add a background, if desired, and color the picture.

Tissue Paper Turkeys
cont.

Directions (*cont.*)
- Apply tissue paper to feather areas, creating a relief effect, by either
    1. placing each piece at the eraser-end of a pencil, pressing it down on all sides around the pencil, dipping the eraser end into the glue while holding the tissue in place, and placing it on the turkey in an appropriate place for feathers; or
    2. rolling each piece into a ball, dipping the ball into the glue, and placing it on the turkey where desired.

Tasting Critique
- Is the overall effect pleasing?
- Are the color choices pleasing?
- Was the work done neatly?
- Was the picture drawn well?

Stirring In the Curriculum
- Use in conjunction with a science unit on the five senses by relating the tissue paper effect to sight and touch.

What Shall We Cook Up Tomorrow?
- Try using this tissue paper technique with other subjects (different holidays, spring flowers, animals, flags, maps, etc.).

COOKIES AND CANDIES
(Holidays and Seasonal Art)

Macaroni Turkeys

Cooking Terms

background	foreground
depth	texture

Ingredients/Utensils
- 12"-x-15" pieces of cardboard (size can vary)
- Pencils
- Crayons
- Marking pens
- Glue
- Macaroni (various shapes)
- Photocopies or pictures depicting a turkey (optional)
- Watercolor paints

Directions
Teacher:
- Discuss the definition *depth* (see "Cooking Principles," page xv).
- Discuss the use of foreground and background.

Student:
- Using a pencil, draw a turkey on a piece of cardboard (if desired, use a photocopy as a guide). You may wish to be creative and "dress" your turkey according to a theme (a baseball player, a ballerina, etc.).

Macaroni Turkeys
cont.

Directions (*cont.*)
- Draw a background (barn, fence, hills, etc.) that is appropriate to the theme of the picture.
- Color the picture using crayons.
- Glue macaroni pieces to the turkey's feathers or to the turkey's body.
- Paint macaroni with watercolors, keeping the paint fairly thick.

Tasting Critique
- Was the turkey drawn well?
- Was the background drawn well?
- Does the picture show depth?

Stirring In the Curriculum
- Use in conjunction with a science unit on the five senses by relating the macaroni effect to sight and touch.
- Use in conjunction with a social science unit on farm animals.
- Refer to *A Turkey for Thanksgiving* by Eve Bunting, in which the turkey is dressed in a vest.

What Shall We Cook Up Tomorrow?
- Macaroni pieces can be used for almost any subject. Be imaginative and see what ideas you can create.

COOKIES AND CANDIES
(Holidays and Seasonal Art)

Winter Scenes

Note: When it's cold outside, this recipe really hits the spot!

Cooking Terms

background	mitten	sleigh
deciduous	scarf	snowman
evergreen	ski	
foreground	ski lift	

Ingredients/Utensils
- 9"-x-12" sheets of blue construction paper
- Oil pastels
- Pencils (optional)

Directions
Teacher:
- Discuss winter subjects and activities (deciduous and evergreen trees, making snowmen, skiing, sledding, etc.).

Student:
- On a sheet of 9"-x-12" blue construction paper, draw a winter scene with oil pastels. (If desired, the picture can be drawn first with pencil.)
- Color the picture with oil pastels.

Winter Scenes
cont.

Tasting Critique
- Does the picture appear to be a winter scene?
- Was the picture drawn and colored well?
- Were the student's ideas original?

Stirring In the Curriculum
- Use in conjunction with a social science unit on winter.
- Refer to *Owl Moon* by Jane Yolen, in which the illustrations depict winter scenes.

What Shall We Cook Up Tomorrow?
- Make snowmen pictures on blue paper using oil pastels. Glue on fabric for the scarf and tape on twigs for the arms and maybe buttons, too!

COOKIES AND CANDIES
(Holidays and Seasonal Art)

Fanned Christmas Trees

Cooking Terms

decorate	relief	three-dimension
ornaments	theme	trim

Ingredients/Utensils

- 9"-x-12" sheets of green construction paper
- Stapler
- Small squares of construction paper for ornaments (colors can vary)
- Scissors
- Crayons
- 9"-x-12" sheets of red construction paper for background (optional)
- Sequins, glitter, and other decorative materials (optional)

Directions

Teacher:

- Discuss creative ways to decorate trees (with candy canes, toys, ribbons, specialty ornaments, Christmas cards, etc.).

Student:

- Fold a sheet of 9"-x-12" green construction paper back and forth, as if to make a fan.
- Pinch one 9" side together to form a triangular shape or fan.

Fanned Christmas Trees
cont.

Directions (*cont.*)
- Staple the tree at the pinched end (the top of the tree).
- Decorate the tree in any manner, using colored construction paper, crayons, and other decorative materials.
- Complete the tree by adding a trunk.
- (Optional) Staple the tree to background paper. Gifts or decorations around the tree may be added on background paper.

Tasting Critique
- Is the finished product attractive?
- Were the student's ideas creative?

Stirring In the Curriculum
- Use in conjunction with a science unit on trees.
- Do a creative writing lesson entitled "My Christmas Tree."
- Study the origins of the Christmas tree.

What Shall We Cook Up Tomorrow?
- Make a smaller fanned tree and glue it on the front of a Christmas card project.
- Use this fan technique to create feathers for art activities involving Thanksgiving turkeys, or simply to make designs by gluing fans on background paper.

COOKIES AND CANDIES
(Holidays and Seasonal Art)

Christmas Living Room Scenes

Cooking Terms

      alternate   depth   perspective

Ingredients/Utensils
- 9"-x-12" or 12"-x-18" sheets of white construction paper (size can vary)
- 4"-x-6" or 6"-x-9" sheets of red construction paper (size can vary)
- Pencils
- White crayons or white chalk
- Scissors
- Glue
- Crayons, colored pencils, or marking pens

Directions

Teacher:
- Discuss indoor Christmas activities (decorating a tree, baking, wrapping gifts, hanging stockings, etc.).
- Discuss the definitions of *depth* and *perspective* (see "Cooking Principles," page xv, and teacher directions, page 16). Encourage students to draw objects at the front, middle, and back of their Christmas living room scenes.

Christmas Living Room Scenes
cont.

Directions (*cont.*)
- Discuss how to draw a fireplace for the Christmas living room scene. Rows of bricks should alternate (*Fig. A*).

Fig. A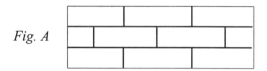

Student:
- Draw a fireplace on red paper by alternating the rows of bricks and tracing lines with white crayon or white chalk.
- Cut out and glue the fireplace onto white paper.
- Draw the remainder of your living room scene.
- Color your picture.

Tasting Critique
- Is there a feeling of depth?
- Was the scene drawn well?
- Were the bricks drawn correctly?
- Were the student's ideas original?

Stirring In the Curriculum
- Use in conjunction with a mathematics unit on measurement or proportion by having students design a room and draw it to scale.
- Refer to *Cecily's Christmas* by Iris Van Rynbach, in which several illustrations depict Christmas living room scenes.

What Shall We Cook Up Tomorrow?
- Try drawing other pictures using bricks (walls, buildings, etc.).

COOKIES AND CANDIES
(Holidays and Seasonal Art)

Spring Flower Arrangements

Cooking Terms

accent	bouquet	petal	three-dimensional
arrange	florist	texture	vase

Ingredients/Utensils

- 9"-x-12" sheets of white construction paper
- Crayons
- Small pieces of construction paper (various sizes and colors)
- Scissors
- Glue

Directions

Teacher:

- Display sample flower arrangements and art prints. It might be helpful to invite a florist to visit and demonstrate flower arranging.

Student:

- Draw a flower container (vase, basket, etc.) on a sheet of white construction paper.
- Draw stems and leaves extending out from the container.

106

Spring Flower Arrangements
cont.

Directions (*cont.*)
- Color the container, stems, and leaves.
- Draw flowers on pieces of colored construction paper. Try to vary the shapes, sizes, and colors of flowers.
- Add crayon to flowers for texture and accent.
- Cut out the flowers and glue them in appropriate places (petals may be folded, without using glue, so they appear three-dimensional).
- If desired, add a table or other background objects.

Tasting Critique
- Is the flower arrangement attractive?
- Was the work done neatly?

Stirring In the Curriculum
- Use in conjunction with a science unit on plants.
- Refer to *Alison's Zinnia* by Anita Lobel, in which the illustrations depict very colorful spring flowers.

What Shall We Cook Up Tomorrow?
- Use colored tissue paper in place of construction paper for flowers (see student directions, page 96).

COOKIES AND CANDIES
(Holidays and Seasonal Art)

Woven Easter Baskets

*Note: This is an excellent fine-motor skills project.
Students seem to really enjoy this one.*

Cooking Terms

horizontal	strips	warp	weft
pattern	vertical	weave	

Ingredients/Utensils

- 9"-x-12" sheets of white paper
- 6"-x-9" sheets of white paper
- 1"-x-6" strips of paper (various colors)
- Glue
- Crayons
- 1" squares of colored tissue paper (optional)
- Scissors

Directions

Teacher:

- Demonstrate the technique for weaving paper.

Student:

- Put a little glue at one end of a paper strip and glue it vertically on a sheet of 6"-x-9" white paper.
- Glue on a second strip in the same manner, next to the first strip.
- Continue until four or five strips are glued to the paper.

Woven Easter Baskets
cont.

Directions (*cont.*)
- Begin weaving the horizontal (or "weft") strips using a basic over-under, over-under pattern.
- Slide each strip toward the glued ends of the vertical (or "warp") strips. (Strips may touch or space may be left between them— see illustration at the beginning of this recipe.)
- Continue until four or five strips are in place.
- Glue down all ends of the strips (horizontal and vertical).
- Cut out a basket shape (*Fig. A*) from the woven strips.

Fig. A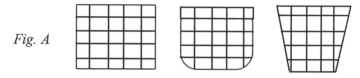

- Glue the basket to the lower end of a sheet of 9"-x-12" white paper.
- Draw and color a handle and eggs.
- (Optional) Apply tissue paper to accent the handle and eggs (see student directions, page 96).
- Add background art, if desired.

Tasting Critique
- Is the overall appearance pleasing?
- Was the weaving done accurately?
- Was the work done neatly?

Stirring In the Curriculum
- Use in conjunction with a social science unit on Native Americans or any other culture known for its basketry.

What Shall We Cook Up Tomorrow?
- Try weaving 1/2" strips.
- To create a different effect, use strips with curved edges.
- Make spring baskets with flowers in place of eggs.

COOKIES AND CANDIES
(Holidays and Seasonal Art)

Sun Pictures

Cooking Terms
character   imagination   ray   sun

Ingredients/Utensils
- 12"-x-18" sheets of black construction paper
- 9"-x-12" sheets of yellow construction paper
- Scissors
- Glue
- Crayons
- 8"- to 9"-diameter paper circles
- Compasses (optional)

Directions
Teacher:
- Discuss various possibilities for sun faces and designs.

Student:
- Cut out an 8"- to 9"-diameter paper circle and trace it onto yellow construction paper (older students can draw their own circles using a compass).
- Cut out the yellow circle.
- Design and color a face. Be creative! (Include a big smile, a hat, sunglasses, freckles, etc.)

Sun Pictures
cont.

Directions (*cont.*)
- Glue the sun face at the center of a sheet of black construction paper.
- Using leftover yellow paper, design sunrays, cut them out, and glue them around the sun.

Tasting Critique
- Were the student's ideas original?
- Was the sun picture drawn well?
- Was the work done neatly?

Stirring In the Curriculum
- Use in conjunction with a science unit on astronomy by studying facts pertaining to the sun.
- Refer to the fable *The North Wind and the Sun* by Jean de La Fontaine, in which the illustrations depict the sun with a face.

What Shall We Cook Up Tomorrow?
- Have students draw sun pictures depicting scenes on a hot day. Then send the pictures to the weather department of your local television station (check with the television station first to see if they will display student artwork on the air).

International Specialties
(Multicultural Art)

INTERNATIONAL SPECIALTIES
(Multicultural Art)

African Circle Art

Cooking Terms

concentric   dominant   tie-dye
converge   overlap

Ingredients/Utensils
- 9"-x- 12" or 12"-x-18" sheets of colored construction paper
- Oil pastels

Directions

Teacher:
- Discuss the tie-dye technique and its influence on African-style clothing.

Student:
- Mark five points on a sheet of construction paper.
- Using an oil pastel, make a ring around the first point, always stroking back and forth toward the point.
- With another color, repeat the previous step, forming a concentric ring that touches the first ring.
- Continue the process, using two or more colors. Move to another point at any time.
- When rings begin to converge, one ring must take precedence.
- Continue until the entire paper is filled.

African Circle Art
cont.

Tasting Critique
- Do all strokes point to the center of each circle?
- Is the paper completely filled?
- Is the overall effect pleasing?

Stirring In the Curriculum
- Use in conjunction with a social science unit on Africa.
- Use in conjunction with a geometry lesson on concentric circles (see teacher directions, page 4).
- Refer to *Batik and Tie-Dye* by Susie O'Reilly, which depicts tie-dye photographs showing the "African Circle Art" technique.

What Shall We Cook Up Tomorrow?
- This technique may be done on a smaller scale for greeting cards or other projects where designs are necessary.

INTERNATIONAL SPECIALTIES
(Multicultural Art)

American Indian Bead Jewelry

*Note: Here's an opportunity for older students
to practice fine-motor skills.*

Cooking Terms

bead	loom	needle	warp	weft
geometric	motif	thread	weave	

Ingredients/Utensils
- Graph paper
- Colored pens, colored pencils, or crayons
- Indian seed beads (available from hobby, toy, and variety stores; or from hobby mail-order catalogs)
- Sewing needles (thin enough to fit through bead holes)
- Thread
- 8 Popsicle™ sticks (or other sticks) for each student, or preassembled looms (available from hobby stores or hobby mail-order catalogs)
- Wood glue

Color Code

- ▨ Red
- ◙ Green
- ▩ Yellow
- ☐ White
- ◕ Black

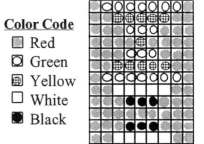

Fig. A

Directions

Teacher:
- Discuss American Indian jewelry (geometric motifs, color, beading technique, etc.).

Student:
I. Designing the pattern.
- Using graph paper and colored pencils, design a geometric pattern (*Fig. A*).

II. Making the loom.
- Glue four sticks together to form a frame (*Fig. B*).

Fig. B

American Indian Bead Jewelry

cont.

Directions (*cont.*)

- Attach four half-sticks vertically, to the tops and bottoms of frame corners (*Fig. C*).
- Glue two sticks, as crossbars, to the top and bottom of the frame (*Fig. D*).

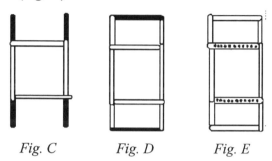

Fig. C   *Fig. D*   *Fig. E*

- Glue a row of eleven beads (any color) 1/8" apart (centered) to the top and bottom of the inner frame (*Fig. E*).
- Cut ten 18" pieces of thread.
- To form the loom, tie ten threads tightly to the centers of the top and bottom of the outer frame (*Fig. F*).
- Separate the threads by lifting each with a needle and placing it between beads at the top and bottom of the inner frame (*Fig. G*).

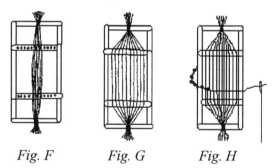

Fig. F   *Fig. G*   *Fig. H*

III. Beading the loom.

- Thread the needle with a single 3' strand of thread.
- Tie the thread to an outside loom thread near the top of the loom.
- Keeping the thread under the loom threads, thread on nine beads for the first row (*Fig. H*).

117

INTERNATIONAL SPECIALTIES
(Multicultural Art)

Directions (*cont.*)

- Pull the thread until beads are below the loom threads, and push up each bead with your finger until it is between two loom threads. Insert the needle through bead holes above the loom threads, a few at a time, until the entire row is held in place. Make sure that each bead is in its proper position (*Fig. I*).

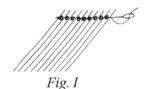

Fig. I

- Straighten the row by pushing beads with a stick.
- Continue beading second and remaining rows in the same manner as first row, following pattern and colors and keeping each row straight and tight against each other (*Fig. J*).

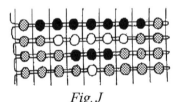

Fig. J

- To complete the beadwork, insert the needle back through several beads of the last row.
- Remove the needle and cut off excess thread.

IV. Removing beadwork from the loom.
- Untie the knots from the frame crossbars.
- Knot all ten threads together at both ends. Or, if desired, make a bead fringe at each end by threading two threads at a time with beads and then knotting the threads (*Fig. K*).

Fig. K

118

American Indian Bead Jewelry
cont.

Directions (*cont.*)

V. Using the finished piece.
- Use the beadwork as a belt decoration, wristband, part of a necklace, hatband, handbag decoration, etc.

Tasting Critique
- Is the design attractive?
- Did the student follow his or her original graph design accurately?
- Was the technique used correctly?

Stirring In the Curriculum
- Use in conjunction with a social science unit on Native Americans.
- Refer to *Indian Beadwork* by Robert Hofsinde, in which the illustrations depict examples of Indian bead jewelry.

What Shall We Cook Up Tomorrow?
- Use more or fewer threads to make a different-sized beadwork piece (bead picture, belt, ring, earrings, etc.).

INTERNATIONAL SPECIALTIES
(Multicultural Art)

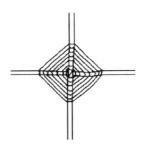

God's Eye Weave

Cooking Terms
    repeat   weave   wrap

Ingredients/Utensils
- Yarn
- Crosses formed from two sticks tied or glued together

Directions
Teacher:
- Prepare crosses.
- Discuss the origin of the God's Eye in Mexican culture. Display examples of God's Eyes.

Student:
- Tie yarn to the center of a cross.
- Hold the cross upright (by its bottom end) in one hand and yarn in the other.
- Wrap yarn completely around the top stick one time (tightly).
- Wrap the yarn around each stick (in order), working either clockwise or counterclockwise, ending back at the top stick.

God's Eye Weave
cont.

Directions *(cont.)*
- Repeat this process until the God's Eye is completed. (To change colors, cut and tie off the existing yarn, then tie on a new color.)
- Tie off the yarn and cut off any excess.

Tasting Critique
- Was the technique done correctly?
- Was a pleasing effect (design) achieved?

Stirring In the Curriculum
- Use in conjunction with a social science unit on Mexico.
- Use in conjunction with a social science lesson on Cinco de Mayo.
- Study the origin of Mexican God's Eyes.

What Shall We Cook Up Tomorrow?
- Try adding tassels at each end of each stick.

INTERNATIONAL SPECIALTIES
(Multicultural Art)

Japanese Fish Painting

Note: My son, Adam, just loves wearing his fish T-shirt.

Cooking Terms

blot	print	texture
fin	scales	

Ingredients/Utensils
- Newsprint or T-shirts
- Large, whole fish (medium to large scales make a better print)
- Printer's ink or tempera paints
- Ink roller
- Paper towels
- Crayons or fabric paints

Directions
Teacher:
- Discuss the history of Japanese fish painting.
- Demonstrate the fish painting technique.
- If you will be doing this recipe with more than one class (and using the same fish), wash off the paint immediately after each lesson.

Japanese Fish Painting
cont.

Directions (*cont.*)

Student:
- With a roller, cover one side of the fish (including fins) with ink or tempera paint. (Do not use too much ink or paint.)
- Blot off excess ink or paint before printing.
- Place newsprint or a T-shirt over the fish (if using a T-shirt, place paper towels inside to protect the back of the shirt) and carefully press the newsprint or shirt against the entire surface of the fish. Be careful not to let the newsprint or the T-shirt slide.
- Carefully remove the newsprint or the T-shirt.
- Add background designs. Use crayons on newsprint or fabric paint on T-shirts.
- Let the fish painting dry.

Tasting Critique
- Was the fish print done well?
- Was the proper amount of ink/paint used?
- Was the background done well?

Stirring In the Curriculum
- Use in conjunction with a social science unit on Japan.
- Use in conjunction with a science unit on fish or ocean life.

What Shall We Cook Up Tomorrow?
- Try doing rubbings using representative textured objects from various cultures.

INTERNATIONAL SPECIALTIES
(Multicultural Art)

An Origami Cup

Note: An excellent recipe for following directions.

Cooking Terms

ancient	fold	opposite
flap	Japanese	origami

Ingredients/Utensils
- Squares of thin paper, preferably origami paper (size and color can vary)

Directions

Teacher:
- Discuss the definition of *origami* (Japanese paper folding).

Student:

Note: When making a fold, always be sure to use a fingernail to crease the fold.

- Fold a square of paper in half diagonally to form a triangle (*Fig. A*).
- Place the triangle in front of you so the fold is toward the bottom (*Fig. B*).
- Fold the lower right corner in until its point reaches the center of the opposite side (*Fig. C*).

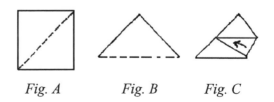

Fig. A   Fig. B   Fig. C

An Origami Cup
cont.

Directions (*cont.*)
- Fold the lower left corner in until its point reaches the center of the opposite side (*Fig. D*).

Fig. D

- Fold down the top flaps in opposite directions (*Fig. E*).
- Spread open the top of the cup (*Fig. F*).

Fig. E   Fig. F

Tasting Critique
- Is the cup able to hold liquid?
- Did the student follow the directions correctly?
- Was the folding done neatly?

Stirring In the Curriculum
- Use in conjunction with a social science unit on Japan.
- Use in conjunction with a language arts lesson by reading *Sadako* and/or *Sadako and the Thousand Paper Cranes* by Eleanor Coerr.

What Shall We Cook Up Tomorrow?
- With the help of a book on origami, make boxes, cranes, puppets, balloons, stars, etc.

INTERNATIONAL SPECIALTIES
(Multicultural Art)

Tube People

Cooking Terms

bodice	proportion	tube
culture	three-dimensional	

Ingredients/Utensils

- Toilet paper or paper towel tubes
- Glue
- Fabric
- Scissors
- Heavy paper such as tagboard or cardboard
- Pencils
- Crayons or marking pens
- Construction paper (optional)
- Odds and ends (buttons, beads, feathers, lace, trim, etc.)

Directions

Teacher:
- Display pictures of people from various cultures or units of study.
- Discuss the possibilities for creating ethnic tube people (Mexico—conquistador; England—queen's guard; Japan—woman wearing a kimono; Africa—tribespeople; etc.).

Tube People
cont.

Directions (*cont.*)
Student:
- Roll tube in glue and cover it with fabric.
- Cut two slits near the top of the tube for arms.
- Using heavy paper or cardboard, draw, color, and cut out head and arms (size should be proportionate to the tube).
- Glue the head to the inside of the tube.
- Slide the arms into the slits.
- Using heavy paper or cardboard, draw, color and cut out a bodice (include jacket, dress, skirt, pants, buttons, lace, belt, scarf, etc.). Fabric may be used for the bodice.
- Glue the bodice to the tube (below the head).
- Draw, color, and cut out legs and feet.
- Glue the legs to the inside of the tube and fold out the feet.
- If desired, make stands for the tube people.

Tasting Critique
- Were the student's ideas original?
- Was the technique used correctly?

Stirring In the Curriculum
- Use in conjunction with a language arts lesson by using the tube people as finger puppets and presenting a puppet show.

What Shall We Cook Up Tomorrow?
- Make tube animals using this technique.

INTERNATIONAL SPECIALTIES
(Multicultural Art)

Multicultural Holiday Hats

Cooking Terms

brim	cylinder	rectangle
crown	interval	tab

Ingredients/Utensils
- 6"-x-24" sheets of construction paper for hat crowns (color can vary)
- 13"-x-13" sheets of construction paper for hat brims (color can vary)
- Pencils
- Compasses (or circle patterns)
- Scissors
- Rulers
- Glue
- Decorations (pom-poms, foil, tissue paper, sequins, glitter, buttons, fringe, yarn, fabric, ribbon, etc.)

Directions

Teacher:
- Display a sample hat. Point out the brim and the crown.

Student:
I. Making the brim.
- Draw (or trace) a 12" circle using a compass (or pattern) on a sheet of 13"-x-13" construction paper.

Multicultural Holiday Hats

cont.

Directions *(cont.)*
- Draw (or trace) a 6" circle using a compass (or pattern) at the center of the 12" circle (*Fig. A*).
- Cut out both circles. Discard the smaller circle, leaving a doughnut shape for the hat brim.

Fig. A

II. Making the crown.
- Using a sheet of 6"-x-24" construction paper (or decrease the length for a shorter crown), fold one long side up about 1" (*Fig. B*).
- Turn down the folded side and smooth it out.
- With a pencil, mark the fold at 1" intervals (*Fig. C*).
- Cut the interval marks up to the fold line (*Fig. D*).

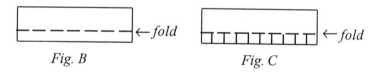

Fig. B   *Fig. C*

- Curl the paper into a cylinder and glue it closed. Fold out the "tabs." *(Fig E)*.
- Put a drop of glue on top of each tab. Place the brim down over the top of the cylinder and press it against the tabs (*Fig. F*).

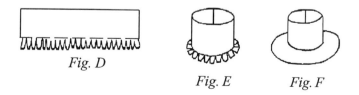

Fig. D   *Fig. E*   *Fig. F*

INTERNATIONAL SPECIALTIES
(Multicultural Art)

Directions (*cont.*)
   III. Decorating the hat.
   - Decide on a multicultural theme for your hat (Cinco de Mayo, Uncle Sam top hat, Irish leprechaun hat, Thanksgiving Pilgrim hat, etc.).
   - Decorate the crown and brim, as desired, with available decorations.

Tasting Critique
   - Can the theme be easily recognized?
   - Does the crown fit well on the brim?
   - Were the student's ideas creative?

Stirring In the Curriculum
   - Incorporate into any language arts, science, or social science unit by using themes or subjects related to your unit of study (U.S. history, presidents, conservation, etc.).

What Shall We Cook Up Tomorrow?
   - Choose other hat themes (party, holiday, occupations, etc.).

INTERNATIONAL SPECIALTIES
(Multicultural Art)

Multicultural Masks

Cooking Terms

ceremony   disguise   papier-mâché

Ingredients/Utensils
- Newspaper
- Wheat paste
- Flat pans
- Scissors
- Paper towels
- Tempera paints
- Paintbrushes
- Paint containers
- Shellac, varnish, or finish spray
- Pieces of cardboard (optional)
- String, hooks, and sticks (optional)

Directions

Teacher:
- Display sample masks or pictures of masks from around the world or from the culture currently under study.
- Discuss the many kinds of masks (religious, ceremonial, theatrical, disguise, holiday, costume, magic, demons, etc.) and what makes certain masks scary.

Multicultural Masks
cont.

Directions (*cont.*)
Student:
- Crumple up large sheets of newspaper to form a flat (2"- or 3"-thick) masklike shape.
- To keep the shape of the mask, bind it with string.
- Tear the newspaper into small strips. Dip them into the wheat paste and apply them to the mask.
- Continue applying the wet strips until three or four layers have been formed. Let the mask dry.
- Cut out eyes and a mouth.
- Form facial features with cardboard or crumpled newspaper.
- Attach facial features to the mask with more wet newspaper strips. Smooth down any edges. Let the mask dry again.
- For a final layer, cover the mask with small, torn pieces of paper towels.
- Paint with tempera paints. Let the paint dry.
- Apply a shiny finish with shellac or varnish.
- (Optional) Display the mask using string, hooks, or sticks.

Tasting Critique
- Is the overall effect pleasing?
- Is the mask smooth (paper edges smoothed down)?
- Were enough layers of papier-mâché applied to make a hard form?
- Was the mask painted well?

Stirring In the Curriculum
- Use in conjunction with a social science unit on any world culture that uses masks.
- Do skits using your masks.
- Refer to *The Mystery of Masks* by Christine Price, which depicts masks from many cultures.

What Shall We Cook Up Tomorrow?
- Try other ideas for papier-mâché projects (dolls, busts, etc.).

MEAL PLANNING (Integrating Art with the Curriculum)

Mon.	Roast Chicken Roast Potatoes Baked Carrots/Green Beans Apple Pie
Tues.	Spaghetti Tossed Salad French Bread Ice Cream and Cookies
Wed.	Beef Stew Biscuits Chocolate Cake
Thu.	Lamb Chops Rice Pilaf Broccoli Strawberry Shortcake
Fri.	Broiled Salmon Baked Potato Peas Tapioca Pudding

MEAL PLANNING
(Integrating Art with the Curriculum)

"About Me" Pictures

Cooking Terms

    fourths   quarters   sections

Ingredients/Utensils
- 12"-x-18" sheets of white paper
- Pencils
- Crayons

Directions

Teacher:
- Discuss possible titles for each of the four sections.

Student:
- Divide a sheet of paper into fourths with pencil.
- Write the title "About Me" at the top of the paper.
- Title each section (e.g., "My Family," "My Favorite Foods," "My Home," "My Room," "My Favorite Things," "My Favorite Place," etc.).

"About Me" Pictures
cont.

Directions (*cont.*)
- Draw an illustration in each box.
- Color each illustration.

Tasting Critique
- Did each illustration support each title?
- Were the illustrations drawn well?
- Were the student's ideas original?

Stirring In the Curriculum
- Incorporate this "four-section" format into any language arts, science, or social science unit by using themes or subjects related to your unit of study (the four seasons, four types of reptiles, etc.).
- Create a "five-section" (or "six-section," etc.) format by incorporating other subjects (favorite books, the continents, the systems of the human body, etc.).
- Have students write about the four titles they selected.

What Shall We Cook Up Tomorrow?
- Do a class mural entitled "About Us."

MEAL PLANNING
(Integrating Art with the Curriculum)

"I Am Thankful for . . ." Turkeys

Cooking Terms

appreciate	thankful
feathers	Thanksgiving

Ingredients/Utensils
- 9"-x-12" sheets of construction paper for backgrounds (color can vary) (optional)
- 9"-x-12" sheets of construction paper for turkeys (color can vary)
- Small pieces of construction paper for feathers (assorted light colors)
- Pencils
- Marking pens
- Scissors
- Glue
- Photocopies or pictures depicting a turkey (optional)
- Photocopies or pictures depicting a feather (optional)

Directions

Teacher:
- Discuss various reasons to be thankful or appreciative.

Student:
- Using a pencil, draw a turkey (without feathers) on a sheet of 9"-x-12" construction paper (if desired, use a photocopy as a guide).

"I am Thankful for ..." Turkeys
cont.

Directions (*cont.*)
- Color the turkey with marking pens.
- Cut out the turkey.
- Draw five to ten feathers on a small sheet of colored construction paper (if desired, use a photocopy as a guide).
- With pencil, write what you are thankful for on each feather ("my family," "my health," "good food," etc.).
- Trace the words with a marking pen.
- Cut out each feather.
- Glue feathers to the turkey.
- (Optional) Glue the turkey to a sheet of 9"-x-12" construction paper (color can vary).

Tasting Critique
- Were creative ideas written on feathers?
- Was the turkey drawn well?
- Was the work done neatly?

Stirring In the Curriculum
- Do a play entitled "The First Thanksgiving."
- Cook an authentic "Pilgrim Feast," which might include turkey (without stuffing), cornbread, nuts, and squash.
- Refer to *The First Thanksgiving* by Jean Craighead George, which depicts beautiful illustrations along with a well-told story.
- Do a creative writing lesson expanding on the ideas on each feather.

What Shall We Cook Up Tomorrow?
- Draw pictures depicting reasons to be thankful.

MEAL PLANNING
(Integrating Art with the Curriculum)

Creature Features

Cooking Terms
creature   monster
imagine   "wild thing"

Ingredients/Utensils
- 9"-x-12" sheets of black construction paper
- Poem or book about a creature or monster
- Pencils
- Oil pastels

Directions
Teacher:
- Read a poem or book to students about creatures or monsters (*Where the Wild Things Are* by Maurice Sendak, *There's a Nightmare in My Closet* by Mercer Mayer, etc.).

Student:
- On a sheet of 9"-x-12" black construction paper, draw an imaginary picture of a creature or monster. Show texture by drawing lines for hair, scales, feathers, and other body features. If desired, include a background.

Creature Features
cont.

Tasting Critique
- Does the creature stand out against the black paper?
- Were imaginative ideas used?
- Was the picture drawn well?

Stirring In the Curriculum
- Have students do a creative writing lesson about their creature entitled "The Day I Went to _____ with My Creature" or "How My Creature Got Its Name."

What Shall We Cook Up Tomorrow?
- Make a class mural by cutting out students' creatures and gluing them on a large sheet of paper. Include a creative background.

MEAL PLANNING
(Integrating Art with the Curriculum)

"There's a _____ Under My Bed"

*Note: This recipe provides plenty of structure
but with lots of room for creativity.*

Cooking Terms

bunk	depth
canopy	imagination

Ingredients/Utensils
- *There's an Alligator Under My Bed* by Mercer Mayer
- 9"-x-12" sheets of white paper
- 2"-x-7" strips of white paper
- Photocopies depicting a bed (side view) with a bedspread
- Scissors
- Tape
- Crayons or marking pens

Directions

Teacher:
- Read to the students *There's an Alligator Under My Bed* by Mercer Mayer.
- Discuss how to draw a bedroom scene and the use of depth (see "Cooking Principles," page xv). Discuss possible objects that may be included in the bedroom scene.

Student:
- On a sheet of 9"-x-12" white paper, using a photocopied image as a guide, draw a side view of a bed (bunk, canopy, etc.) with a bedspread.

"There's a _____ Under My Bed"

cont.

Directions (*cont.*)

- Cut the bedspread picture so that one side opens up with the fold along the top edge (*Fig. A*).

Fig. A

- Turn the picture over and tape a paper strip over the opening.
- On the front side, draw an original picture on the paper strip beneath the bedspread flap (animal, toys, monster, person, shoes, etc.). Be creative and use your imagination (*Fig. B*).

Fig. B

- Draw a background to complete the bedroom scene. Include a dresser, rug, end table, lamp, window, desk, chair, and other bedroom items.

MEAL PLANNING
(Integrating Art with the Curriculum)

Tasting Critique
- Were the student's ideas original?
- Was the picture drawn well?

Stirring In the Curriculum
- Do a creative writing lesson entitled "Help! There's a
_____ Under My Bed" or "How _____ Got
Under My Bed."

What Shall We Cook Up Tomorrow?
- Read *There's a Nightmare in My Closet* by Mercer Mayer and,
instead of a bed, use a closet that opens.

MEAL PLANNING
(Integrating Art with the Curriculum)

Scroll Theaters

Note: This recipe is great for developing oral language skills.

Cooking Terms
> dowel   frame   scroll

Ingredients/Utensils
- Rolled butcher paper (7–9 feet per student)
- Pencils
- Rulers
- Matt knife
- Crayons or marking pens
- Cardboard boxes (size can vary)
- Scissors
- Masking tape
- Wooden dowels (two per student)
- 2"-wide strips of cardboard (cut to the lengths of the boxes)
- 2"-square pieces of cardboard (two per student).

Directions
Teacher:
- Have students write a story that can be illustrated in a series of scenes. (You may wish to have students write their stories *after* their scroll theaters are completed.)

Student:
- Using a ruler, draw a screen on the front of a cardboard box (the size of the screen will vary with the size of the box—see *Fig. A*).

146

Scroll Theaters
cont.

Directions (*cont.*)

- Cut out the screen using a matt knife; set the screen aside. (The teacher may do this step.)
- Cut a sheet of butcher paper (height should be a little less than box height and length should be long enough for desired number of screen frames, including about 2" between each frame).
- Measure the distance from the bottom of the box to the lower end of the screen (*Fig. A*).
- Place the cutout screen about 6" from the left edge of the butcher paper (*Fig. B*).

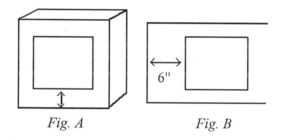

Fig. A   Fig. B

- Trace the screen onto the butcher paper several times, remembering to leave 2" between each frame (*Fig. C*).

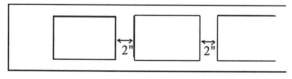

Fig. C

- Write the title of your story on the first frame.
- Begin drawing the story illustrations on the second frame.
- Continue tracing screens and drawing illustrations on each frame until the story is complete. Cut off excess butcher paper, if necessary.
- Color each illustration.

MEAL PLANNING
(Integrating Art with the Curriculum)

Directions (*cont.*)
- Cut the wooden dowels so they are about 2" longer than the height of the box.
- Tape a dowel to one end of the butcher paper so that the illustrations are on the outside when rolled clockwise (*Fig. D*).

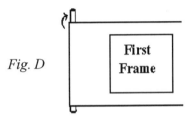

Fig. D

First
Frame

- Turn the dowel clockwise to reach the first frame.
- To complete the scroll, tape the other end of the butcher paper to the second dowel and turn the dowel counter-clockwise (*Fig. E*).

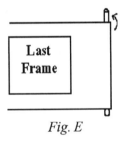

Last
Frame

Fig. E

- Using masking tape, attach two 2" square pieces of cardboard to the inside of the box at the bottom corners—to the right and left of the screen (*Fig. F*).

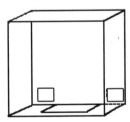

Fig. F (aerial view)

Scroll Theaters
cont.

- Make a hole (to fit the dowel) in the center of each piece of cardboard.
- Tape a cardboard strip to the top of the box directly above the cardboard squares (*Fig. G*). This will help hold the dowels in place.

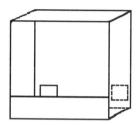

Fig. G (aerial view)

- Make two holes in the cardboard strip directly above the holes in the cardboard pieces.
- Insert dowels with scroll attached, under and through holes in the cardboard strip and into holes into the cardboard squares at the bottom of the box. (*Fig. H*).
- Turn the dowels to operate the scroll theater.

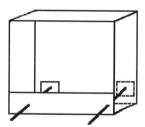

Fig. H (aerial view)

Tasting Critique
- Are the illustrations well correlated with the story?
- Can each picture frame be seen on the screen?
- Were the illustrations drawn well?

MEAL PLANNING
(Integrating Art with the Curriculum)

Stirring In the Curriculum
- Incorporate into any language arts, science, or social science unit by using themes or subjects related to your unit of study (colonial life in America, the westward movement, animals, etc.).
- Have students tell their story to the class and, perhaps, even to other classes.

What Shall We Cook Up Tomorrow?
- Do a class scroll theater in which each student or pair of students is assigned a frame.

MEAL PLANNING
(Integrating Art with the Curriculum)

FractionArt

Cooking Terms

fraction	one-fourth	one-third	shape
measure	one-half	overlap	square
one-eighth	one-sixth	rectangle	triangle

Ingredients/Utensils
- 9"-x-12" or 12"-x-15" sheets of paper (type and color can vary)
- 6"-x-6" sheets of colored paper (type can vary)
- Pencils
- Scissors
- Glue
- Rulers

Directions

Teacher:
- Discuss fractions by using shapes.
- Show how rectangles and triangles can be formed from squares (*Fig. A*).

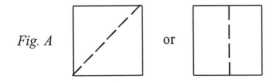

Fig. A   or

Fraction Art

cont.

Directions (*cont.*)

- Show how a square can be divided to create fractions (*Fig. B*).

Fig. B

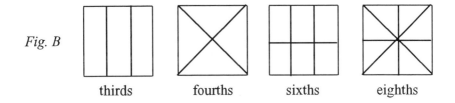

thirds   fourths   sixths   eighths

Student:

- Using 6" squares, measure and cut them into halves, fourths, thirds, sixths, eighths, and so on to form smaller rectangles, squares, or triangles.
- Glue the shapes onto sheets of 9"-x-12" or 12"-x-15" paper to form a desired design (shapes may overlap).

Tasting Critique

- Is the design attractive?
- Were the shapes measured and cut accurately?

Stirring In the Curriculum

- Brainstorm fraction concepts in the real world ("2/3 of the class are girls," "3/4 of the population live in cities," "5/6 of the pie was eaten," etc.).

What Shall We Cook Up Tomorrow?

- Introduce the concept of diameter. Use circles in place of squares to make designs.

MEAL PLANNING
(Integrating Art with the Curriculum)

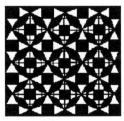

Pattern Art

Cooking Terms
graph   repeat pattern   horizontal   vertical

Ingredients/Utensils
- Photocopies of a square made up of 100 3/4" squares (10 squares x10 squares)
- Pencils
- Marking pens

Directions
Teacher:
- Discuss the concept of repeat patterns.
- Tell students the basic pattern they will be using is square-triangle-triangle or square-"x".
- Have students number their squares from 1–10 along the top horizontal axis and from A–J along the left vertical axis (*Fig. A*).

Student:
- Using a pencil, outline square A-1.
- Draw a triangle in square A-2 and another in square A-3 so that an *X* is formed across squares A-2 and A-3 (*Fig. A*).
- Continue drawing this pattern of square-triangle-triangle (or square-"x") across row A (*Fig. A*).
- Repeat this pattern across rows D,G, and J.
- Repeat this pattern vertically down columns 1, 4, 7, and 10.

Fig. A

Pattern Art
cont.

Directions (*cont.*)
- Notice the nine octagonal shapes that have been formed (*Fig. A*).
- Draw a star by making a 3/4" square in the center of squares B-2, B-3, C-2, and C-3 (*Fig. B*).

Fig. B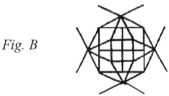

- Draw a triangle on each side of the square so that a vertex touches the center of an *X* (*Fig. B*).
- Draw eight more stars inside the remaining octagonal shapes.
- Color the entire design using marking pens. Use any colors as long as they repeat in some way. There are endless possibilities!
- Cut out the design and frame or mount it. These look great laminated.

Tasting Critique
- Does the color pattern repeat?
- Did the student draw the pattern correctly?
- Was it done neatly?

Stirring In the Curriculum
- Use in conjunction with a mathematics lesson on patterns, sets, geometry, and so on.
- Brainstorm on patterns in the real world (animal patterns, fabric patterns, skyscraper windows, etc.).
- Refer to *Dots, Spots, Speckles, and Stripes* by Tana Hoban, which depicts everyday objects that have patterns.

What Shall We Cook Up Tomorrow?
- Using the photocopy, try having students create their own patterns.

MEAL PLANNING
(Integrating Art with the Curriculum)

Underwater Scenes

Cooking Terms

background	foreground	transparent
contrast	opaque	wash
depth	resist	

Ingredients/Utensils

- 9"-x-12" or 12"-x-18" sheets of white paper
- Blue watercolor paints
- Paintbrushes
- Crayons
- Water containers
- Pencils

Directions

Teacher:

- Discuss various types of sea life (plants, fish, scavengers, shells, coral, etc.).

Student:

- Draw a picture with a pencil on a sheet of white paper. Use depth by including a foreground and a background, and by varying the size of objects.
- Pressing hard with crayons, color all objects. Try to use lots of light colors (white, yellow, orange, pink, green, etc.).
- Using blue watercolor paint, paint a wash over the entire paper to represent water. The crayon areas should resist the paint, creating an effective contrast between the sea life and the water.

156

Underwater Scenes
cont.

Tasting Critique
- Did the student use good composition?
- Can the "crayon-resist" effect be noticed?
- Does the picture depict appropriate sea life?
- Was the picture drawn well?

Stirring In the Curriculum
- Incorporate this "crayon-resist" technique into any language arts, science, or social science unit by using themes or subjects related to your unit of study (black paint over "Outer Space" pictures, blue paint over "Things That Fly" pictures, etc.).
- Refer to *Dive to the Coral Reefs* by Elizabeth Tayntor, Paul Erickson, and Les Kaufman, in which photographs depict a colorful variety of ocean life subjects.

What Shall We Cook Up Tomorrow?
- Create underwater scenes using watercolor paints without crayon.
- Create underwater scenes using other media (beans, macaroni, tissue paper, etc.).

MEAL PLANNING
(Integrating Art with the Curriculum)

Crayon-Rubbing Leaf Prints

*Note: This recipe integrates nicely
with language arts or science.*

Cooking Terms

nature	print	senses
pattern	rub	vein

Ingredients/Utensils
- Thin drawing paper (size can vary)
- Construction paper (color can vary)
- Crayons
- Variety of fresh leaves
- Scissors
- Glue

Directions

Teacher:
- Discuss shapes, colors, and parts of leaves.
- Discuss leaves in relation to the senses.
- If possible, take students on a leaf-hunting walk to observe and gather leaves.

Crayon-Rubbing Leaf Prints

cont.

Directions (*cont.*)
Student:
- Place a leaf or leaves, vein side up, under a sheet of drawing paper.
- Rub crayon across the paper to make prints (rub about 1/4" past the edges of the leaf). Rub in one direction to keep the leaf from slipping.
- Cut out prints and mount them with glue on a sheet of colored construction paper.

Tasting Critique
- Can the veins and texture be seen in each print?
- Were the rubbings done neatly?

Stirring In the Curriculum
- Use in conjunction with a science unit on plants.
- Do a creative writing lesson related to nature (write stories, poems, couplets, similes, etc.).
- Make charts listing the types of leaves used or found on the walk.
- Refer to *How to Make Rubbings* by Michael Kingsley Skinner, which gives ideas for rubbings.

What Shall We Cook Up Tomorrow?
- Make a class mural or collage using leaf prints.

Bibliography

Anno, Mitsumasa. *Anno's Italy*. New York: Collins, 1978.

———. *Upside-Downers*. New York: Walker/Weatherhill, 1971.

Blades, Ann. *Fall*. New York: Lothrop, Lee & Shepard, 1989.

Bunting, Eve. *A Turkey for Thanksgiving*. New York: Clarion Books, 1991.

Coerr, Eleanor. *Sadako and the Thousand Paper Cranes*. New York: G.P. Putnam's Sons, 1977.

Coerr, Eleanor, and Ed Young. *Sadako*. New York: Putnam, 1993.

Constantine, Elizabeth, and Lewis Krevolin. *Ceramics*. New York: Pitman, 1967.

George, Jean Craighead. *The First Thanksgiving*. New York: Philomel Books, 1993.

Goble, Paul. *Crow Chief*. New York: Orchard Books, 1992.

Guback, Georgia. *The Carolers*. New York: Greenwillow Books, 1992.

Hoban, Tana. *Dots, Spots, Speckles, and Stripes*. New York: Greenwillow Books, 1987.

———. *Is It Rough? Is It Smooth? Is It Shiny?* New York: Greenwillow Books, 1984.

———. *Round & Round & Round*. New York: Greenwillow Books, 1983.

Hofsinde, Robert. *Indian Beadwork*. New York: Morrow, 1958.

Johnson, Crockett. *Harold and the Purple Crayon*. New York; Evanston, Ill.: Harper & Row, 1955.

Jonas, Ann. *Color Dance*. New York: Greenwillow Books, 1989.

———. *Round Trip*. New York: Greenwillow Books, 1983.

Keats, Ezra Jack. *Whistle for Willie*. New York: Viking Press, 1964.

Kindred, Wendy. *Ida's Idea*. New York: McGraw-Hill, 1972.

La Fontaine, Jean de. *The North Wind and the Sun*. New York: Franklin Watts, 1964.

Lionni, Leo. *Six Crows*. New York: Knopf, 1988.

Lobel, Anita. *Alison's Zinnia*. New York: Greenwillow Books, 1990.

Lorch, Adolf. *Modern Geometric Design*. New York: Sterling, 1970.

Mayer, Mercer. *There's a Nightmare in My Closet*. New York: Dial Press, 1968.

———. *There's an Alligator Under My Bed*. New York: Dial Books for Young Readers, 1987.

O'Reilly, Susie. *Batik and Tie-Dye*. New York: Thomson Learning, 1993.

Price, Christine. *The Mystery of Masks*. New York: Charles Scribner's Sons, 1978.

Raboff, Ernest. Art for Children Series. New York: Harper & Row; J.B. Lippincott, 1970–1988.

Sendak, Maurice. *Where the Wild Things Are*. New York: Harper & Row, 1963.

Skinner, Michael Kingsley. *How to Make Rubbings*. New York: Van Nostrand Reinhold, 1972.

Tafuri, Nancy. *Follow Me!* New York: Greenwillow Books, 1990.

Taylor, Paul D. *Fossil*. Eye Witness Series. New York: Alfred A. Knopf, 1990.

Tayntor, Elizabeth, Paul Erickson, and Les Kaufman. *Dive to the Coral Reefs*. New York: Crown, 1986.

Te Kanawa, Kiri. *Land of the Long White Cloud: Maori Myths, Tales and Legends*. New York: Arcade, 1989.

Tejima, Keizaburo. *The Bear's Autumn*. La Jolla, Calif.: Green Tiger Press, 1986.

———. *Fox's Dream*. New York: Philomel Books, 1987.

———. *Owl Lake*. New York: Philomel Books, 1987.

———. *Woodpecker Forest*. New York: Philomel Books, 1989.

Testa, Fulvio. *Wolf's Favor*. New York: Dial Books for Young Readers, 1986.

Van Allsburg, Chris. *The Garden of Abdul Gasazi*. Boston: Houghton Mifflin, 1979.

Van Rynbach, Iris. *Cecily's Christmas*. New York: Greenwillow Books, 1988.

Venezia, Mike. Getting to Know the World's Greatest Artists Series. Chicago: Children's Press, 1985–1993.

Walsh, Ellen. *Mouse Paint*. San Diego, Calif.: Harcourt Brace Jovanovich, 1989.

Wisniewski, David. *Sundiata: Lion King of Mali*. New York: Clarion Books, 1992.

Wright, Lyndie. *Puppets*. New York: Franklin Watts, 1989.

Yolen, Jane. *Owl Moon*. New York: Philomel Books, 1987.

Activity Index

About the Author

Linda Arons lives in Oakland, California, with her sons Adam and Micah, where she uses art and children's literature to teach language arts. She enjoys coordinating displays and has exhibited several at the Oakland Unified School District administrative offices. More recently, she presented a stitchery exhibit as part of an ongoing children's art program at San Francisco International Airport. This past year, she developed a "Sister Schools" project, which has been targeted for the Oakland Unified School District to encourage communication and education between their

schools. Currently, Linda is developing a project, entitled "What Worked for Us," that encourages the sharing of ideas among teachers.

Linda has been an educator for twenty-five years. She received a B.A. degree in Design from the University of California, Berkeley in 1967 and a teaching credential from California State University, Hayward in 1969. She has done both classroom and art specialty teaching at elementary and junior high school levels. Her experience in teaching art lessons during fifty-minute class periods has inspired her to develop the quick and easy lessons in *Art Projects Made Easy: Recipes for Fun.*